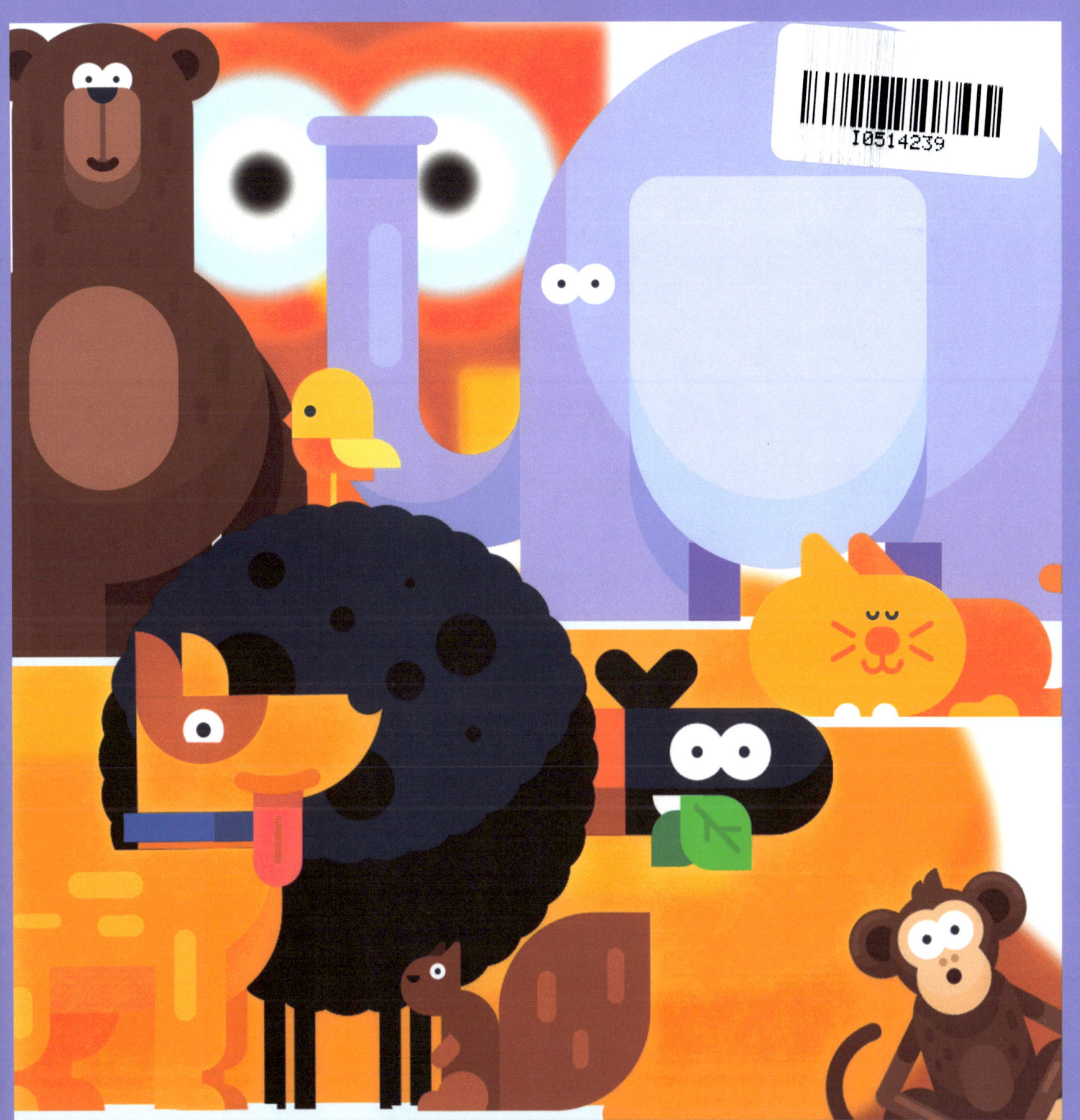

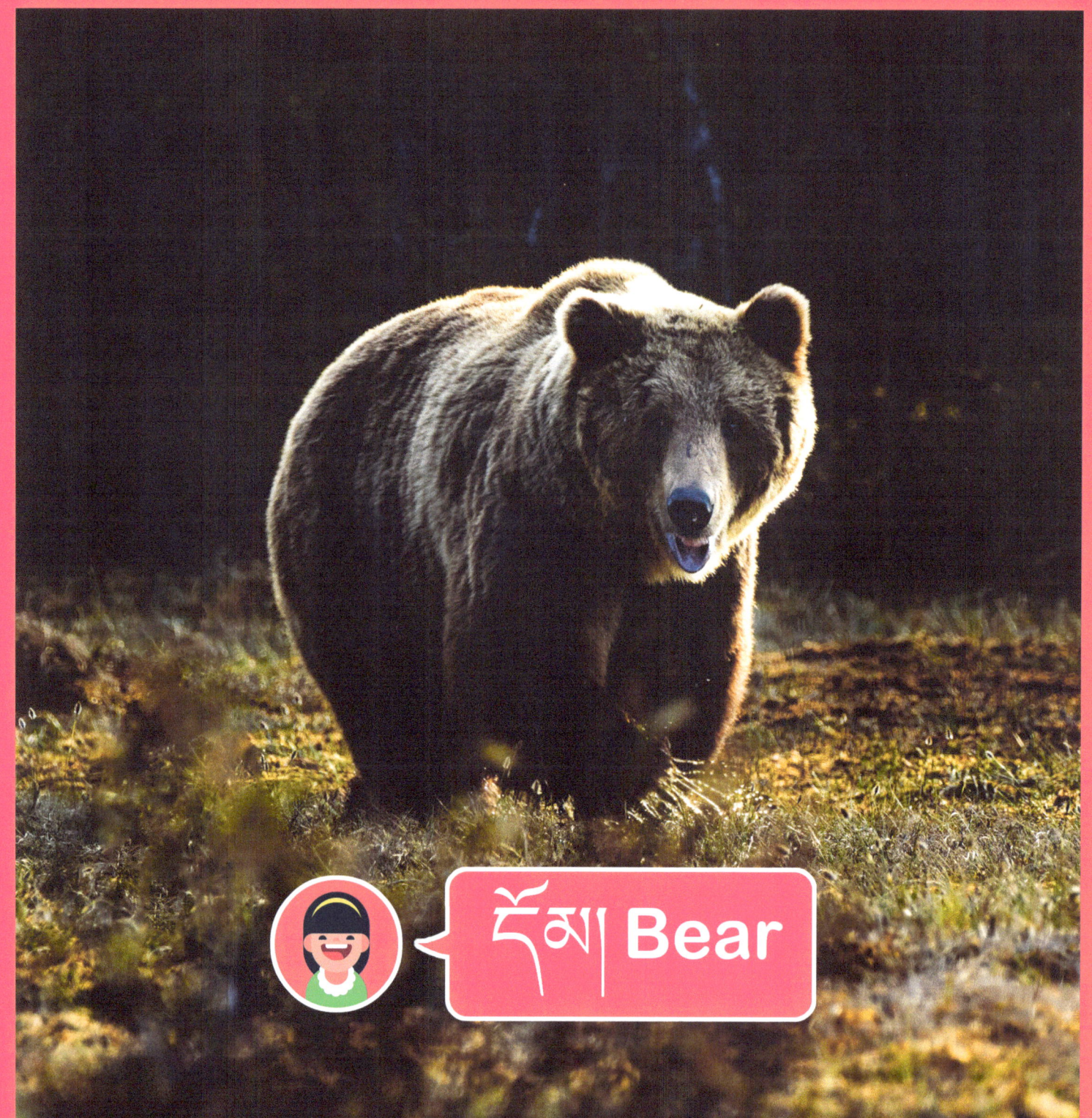

དོམ་ Bear

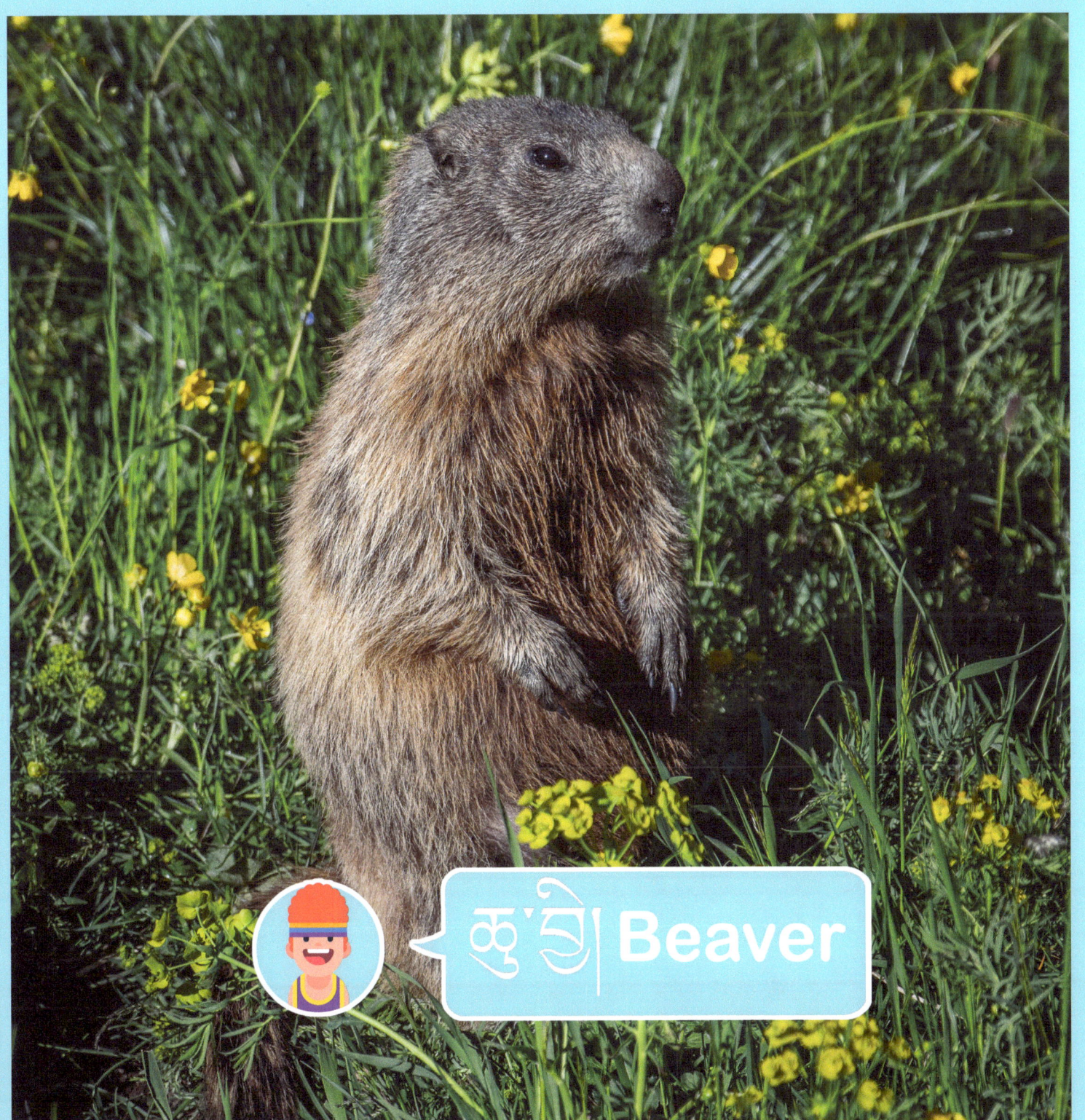
ཆུ་གྲི། Beaver

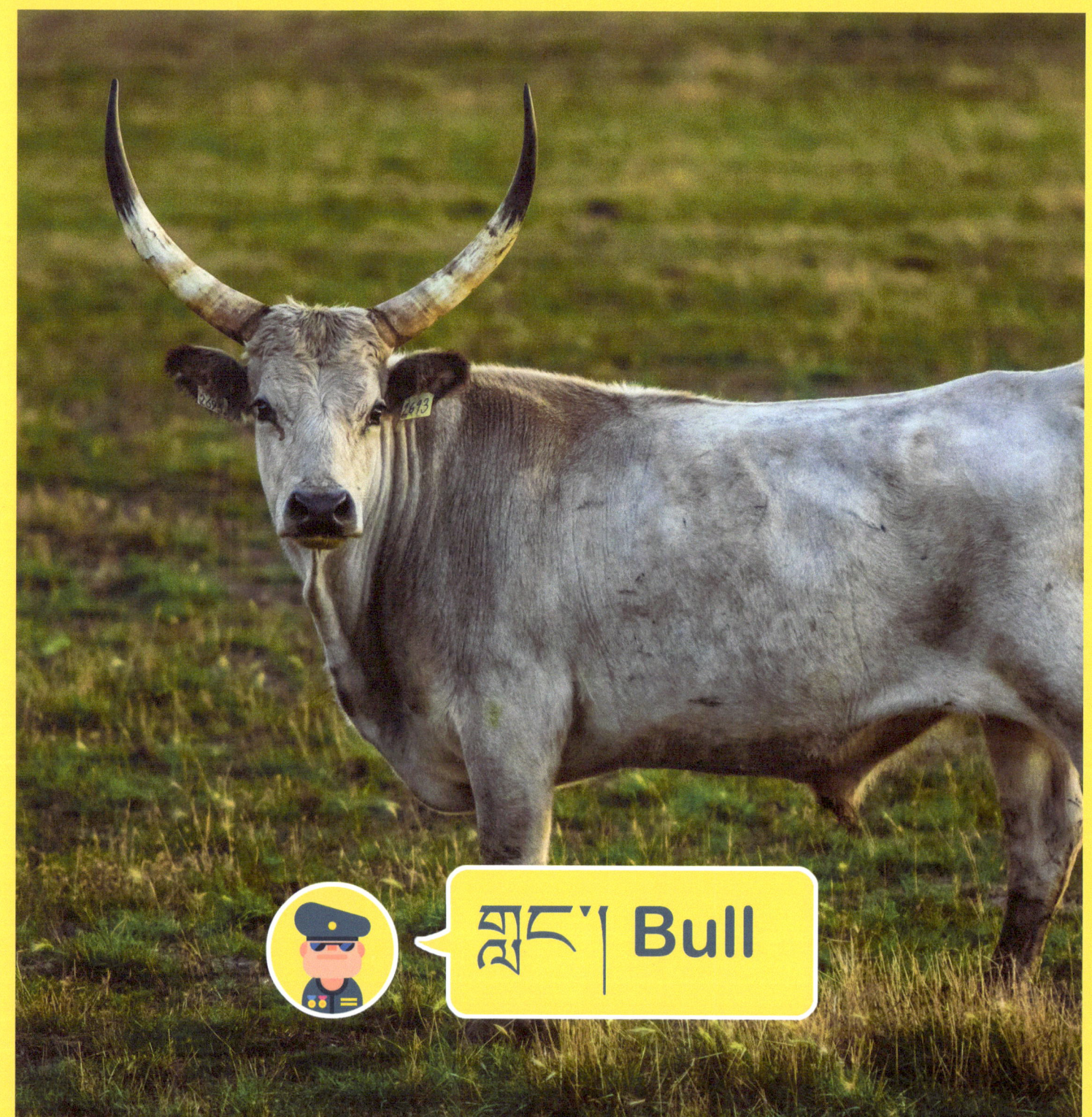

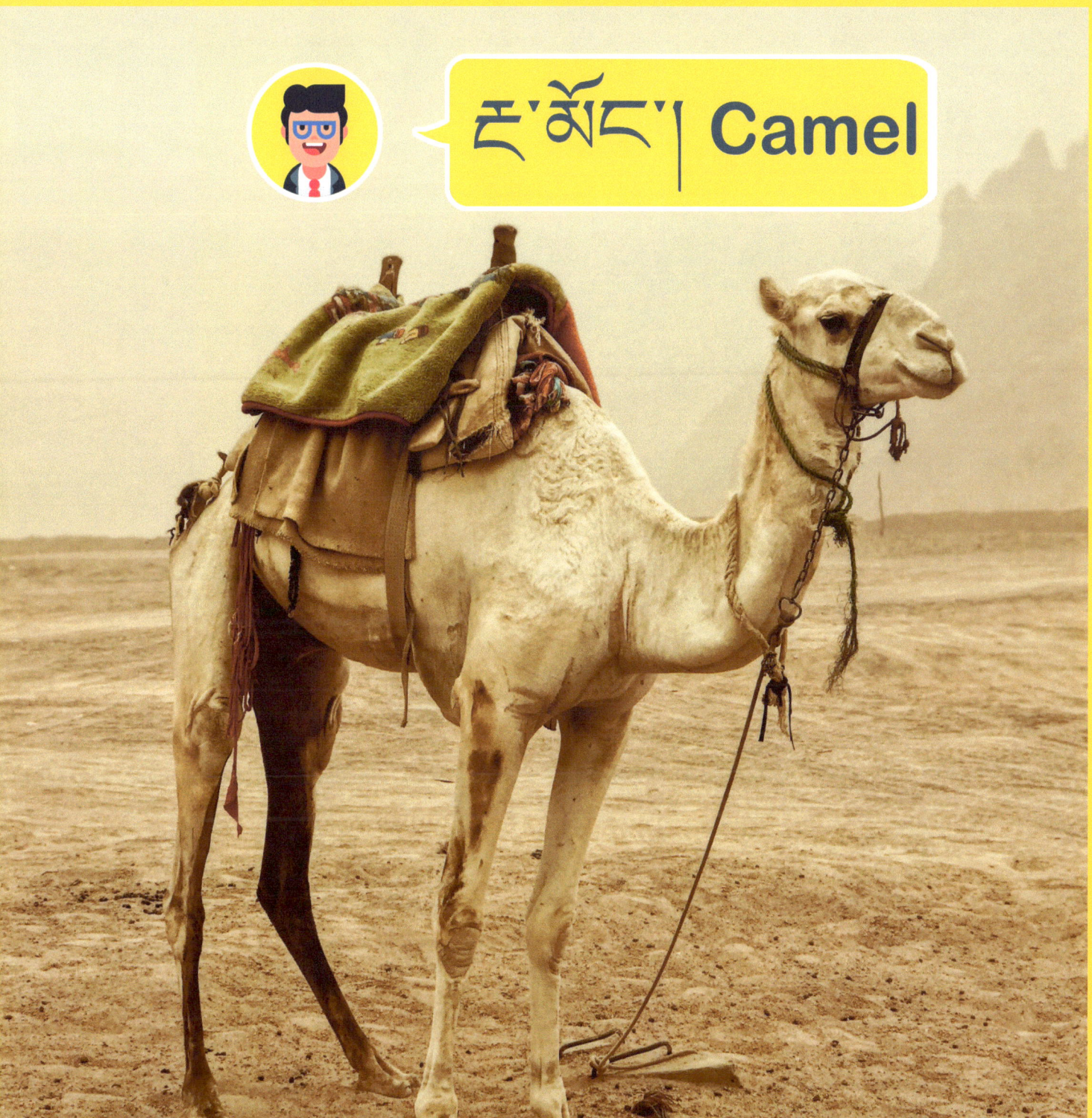

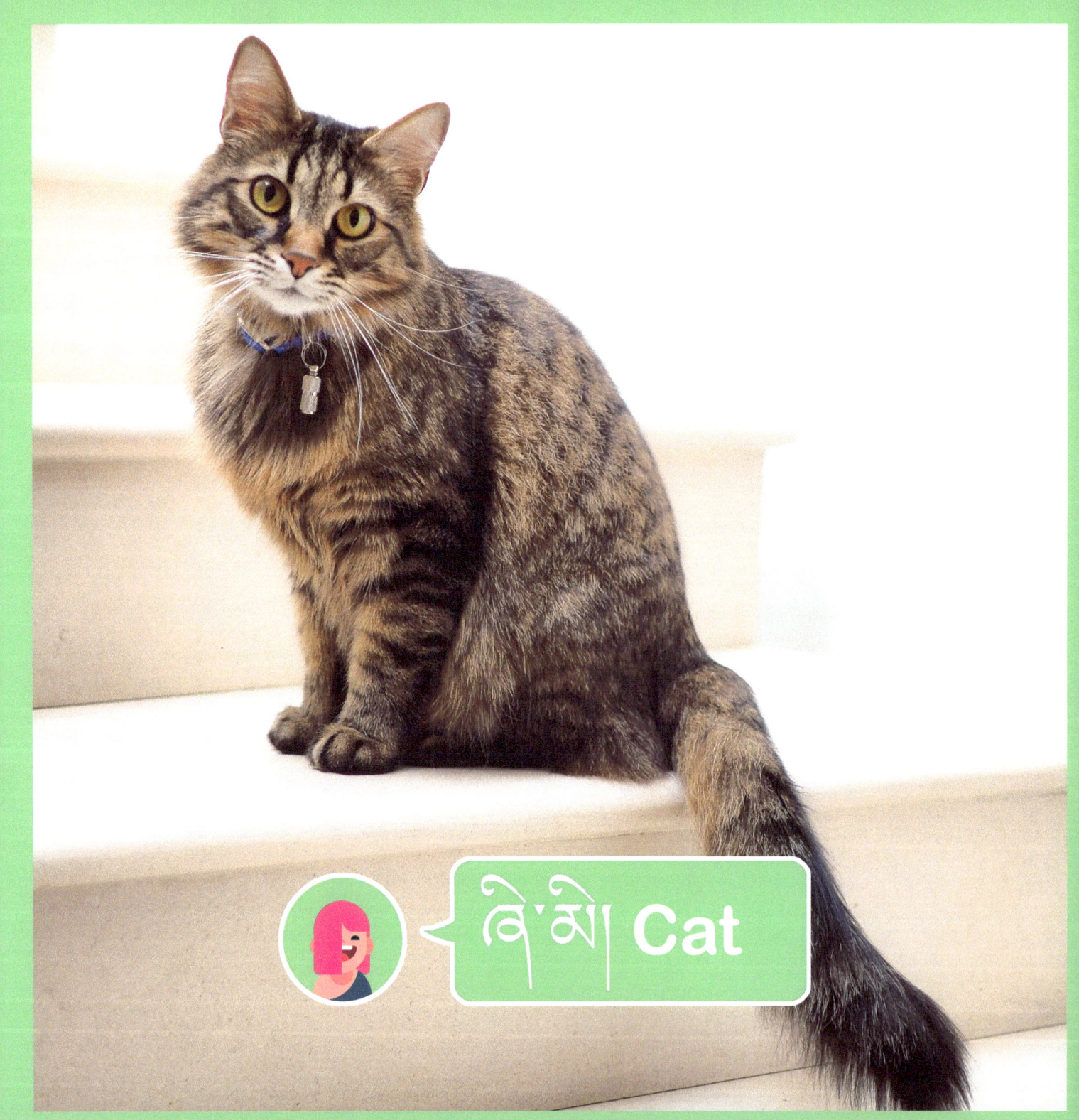

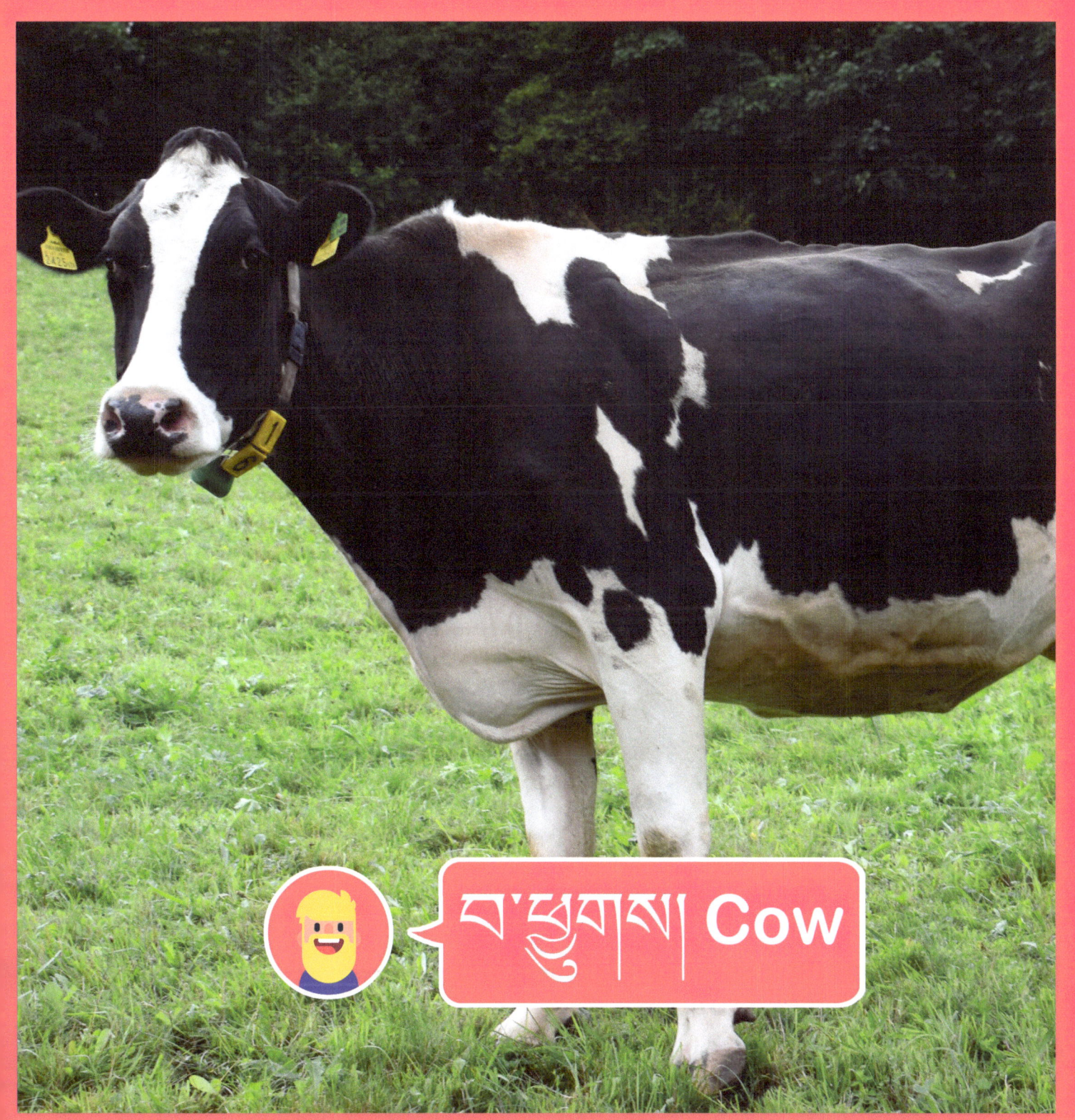

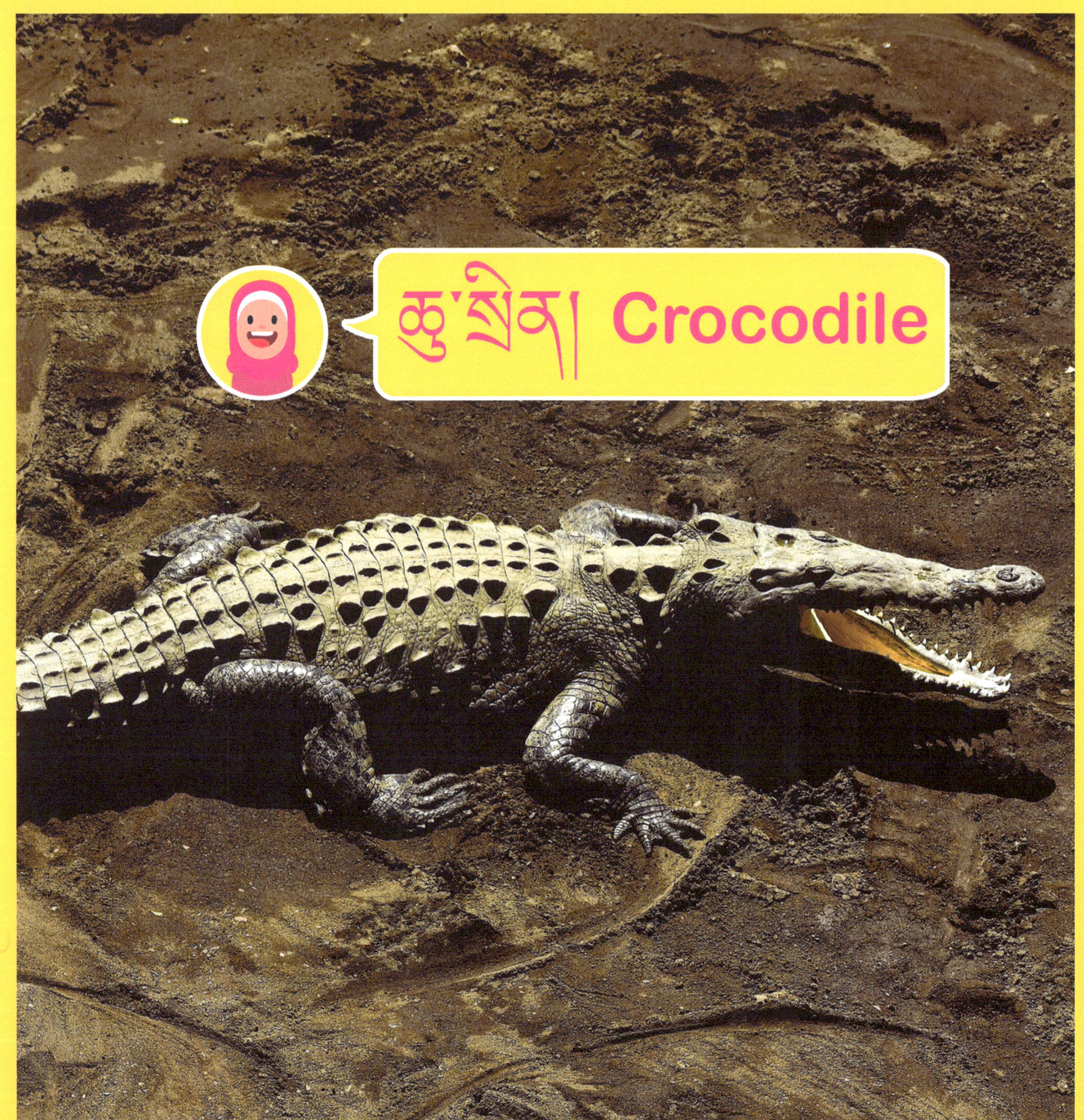

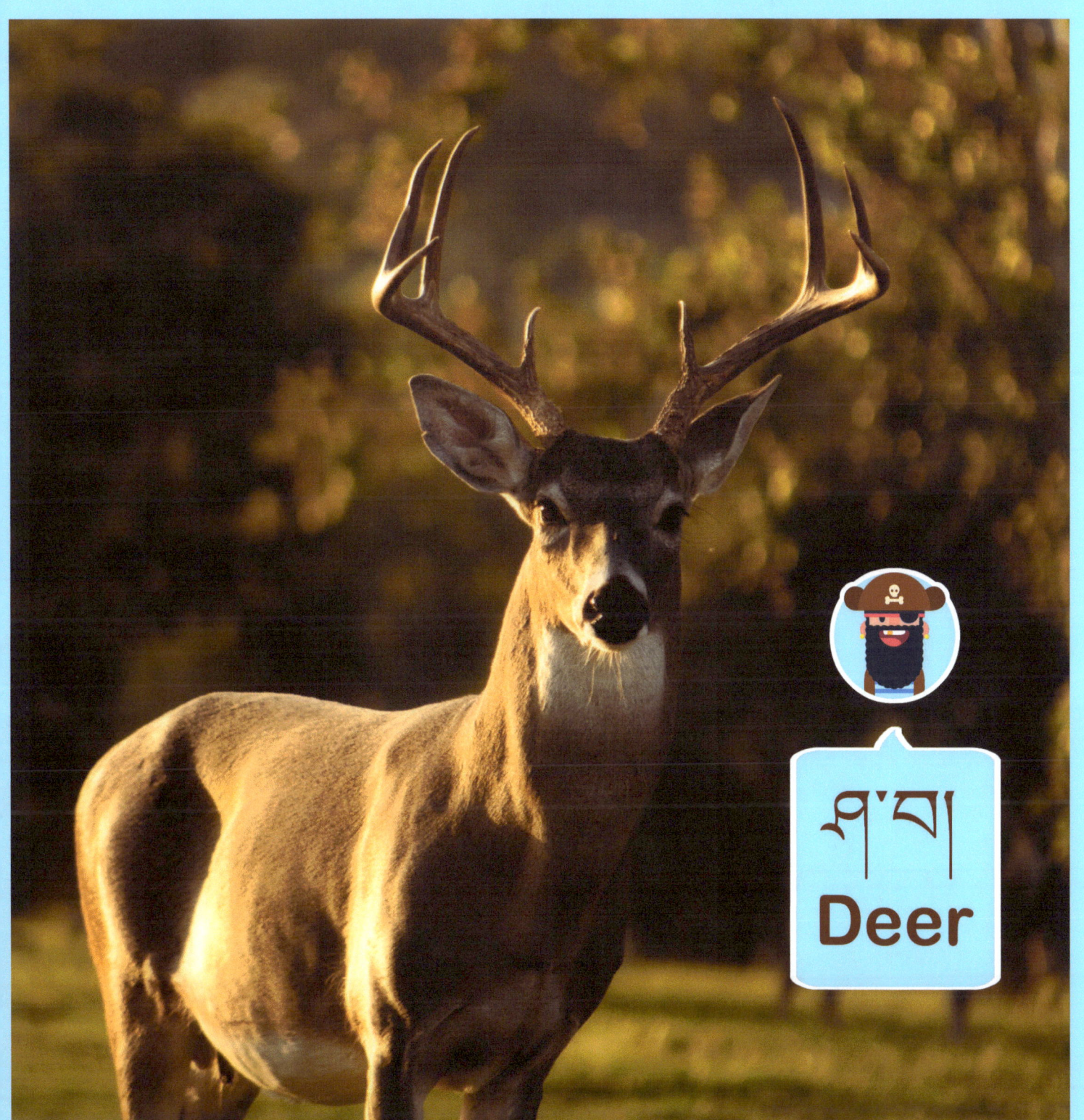

ཤ་བ།
Deer

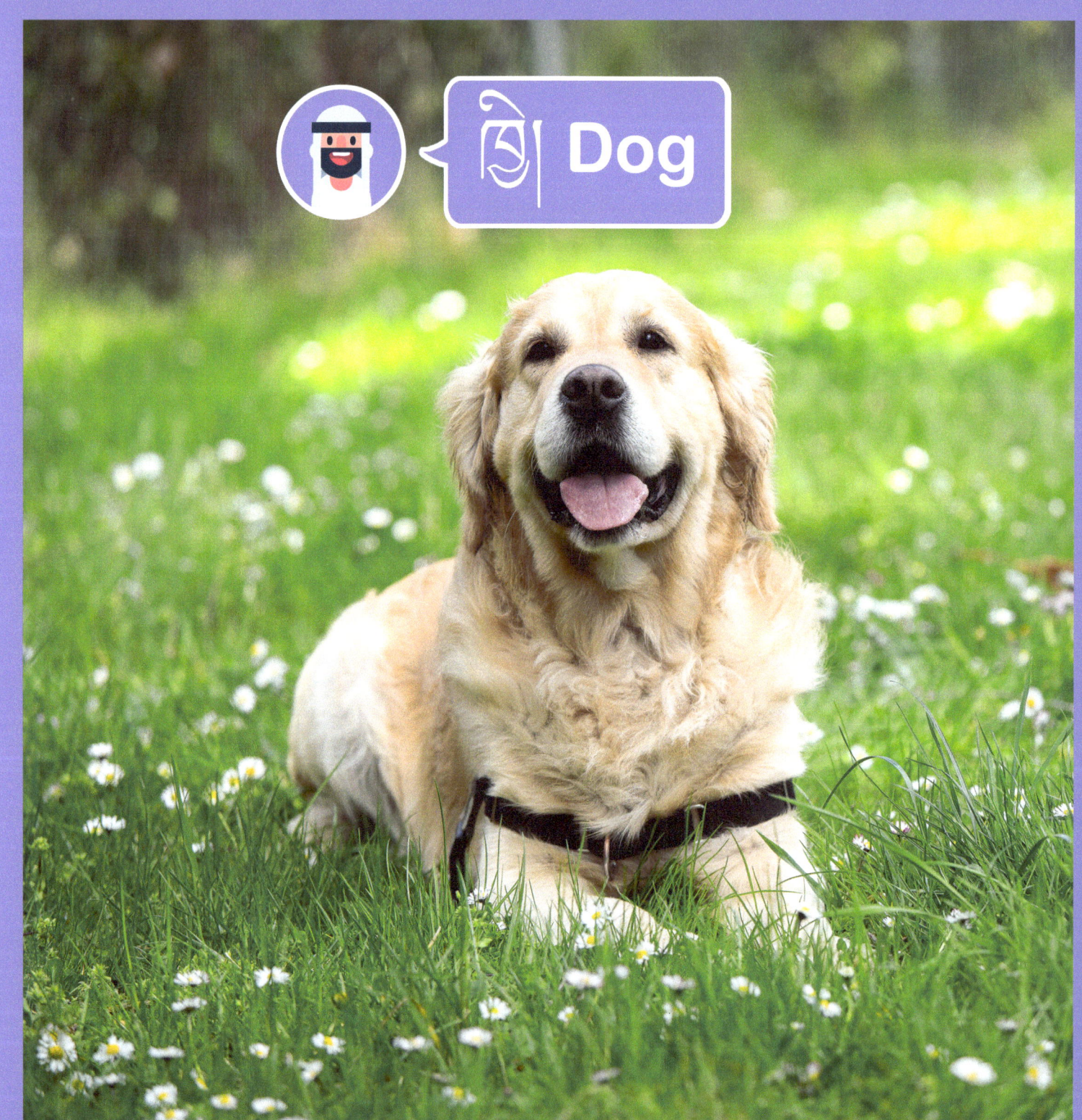

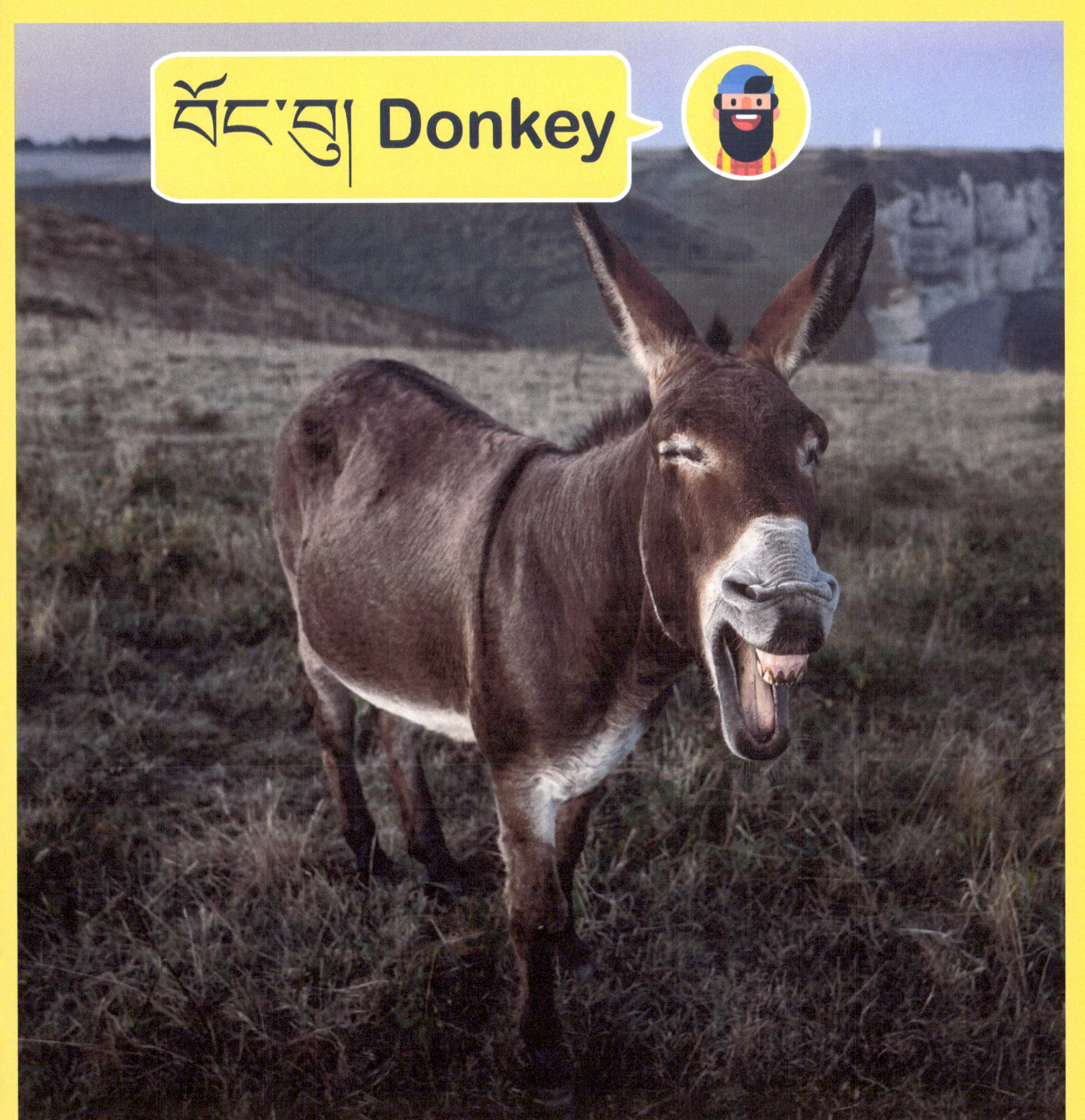

བོང་བུ། Donkey

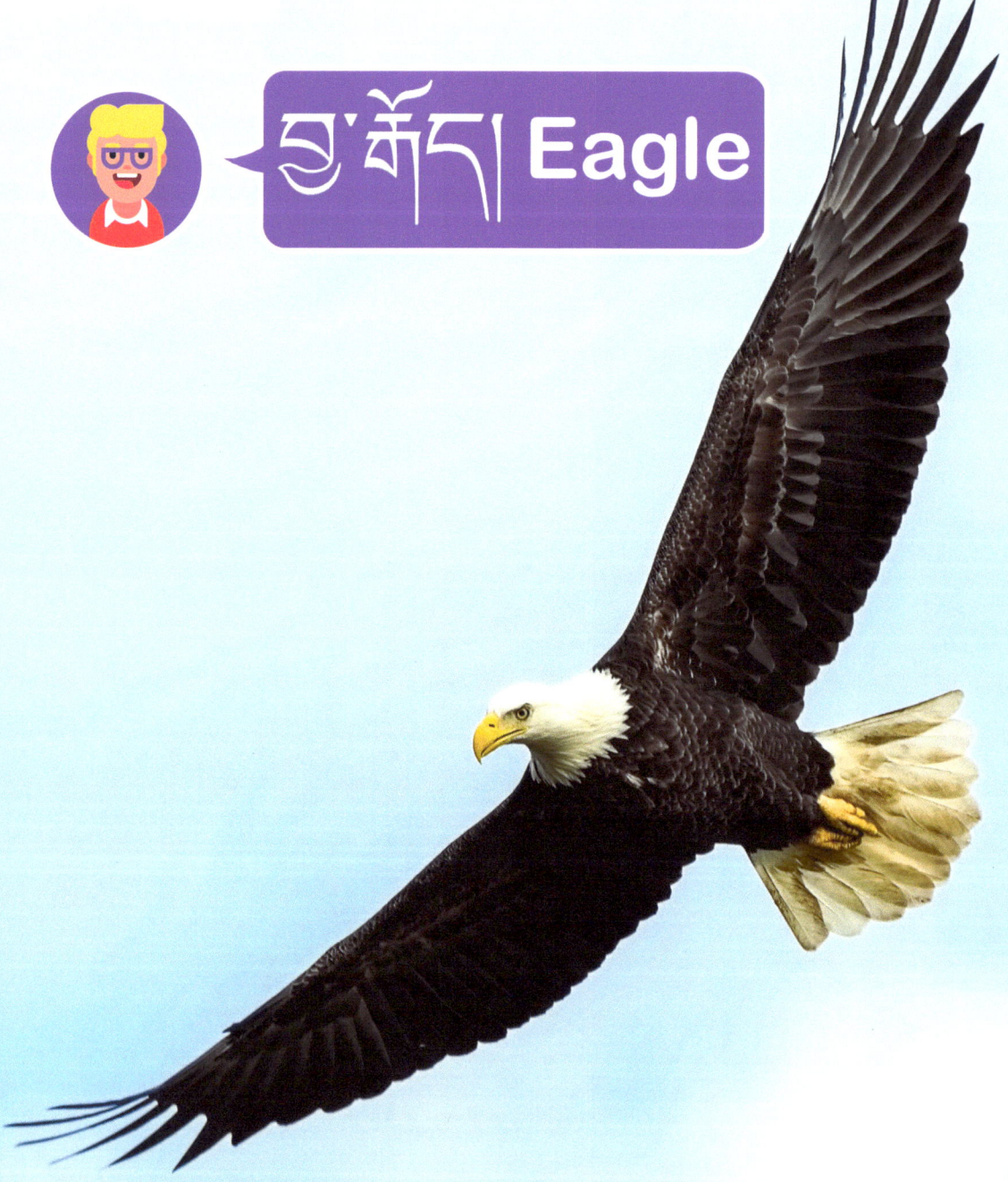

བྱ་རྒོད། Eagle

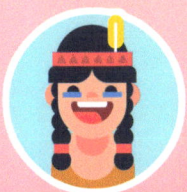 གླང་ཆེན། Elephant

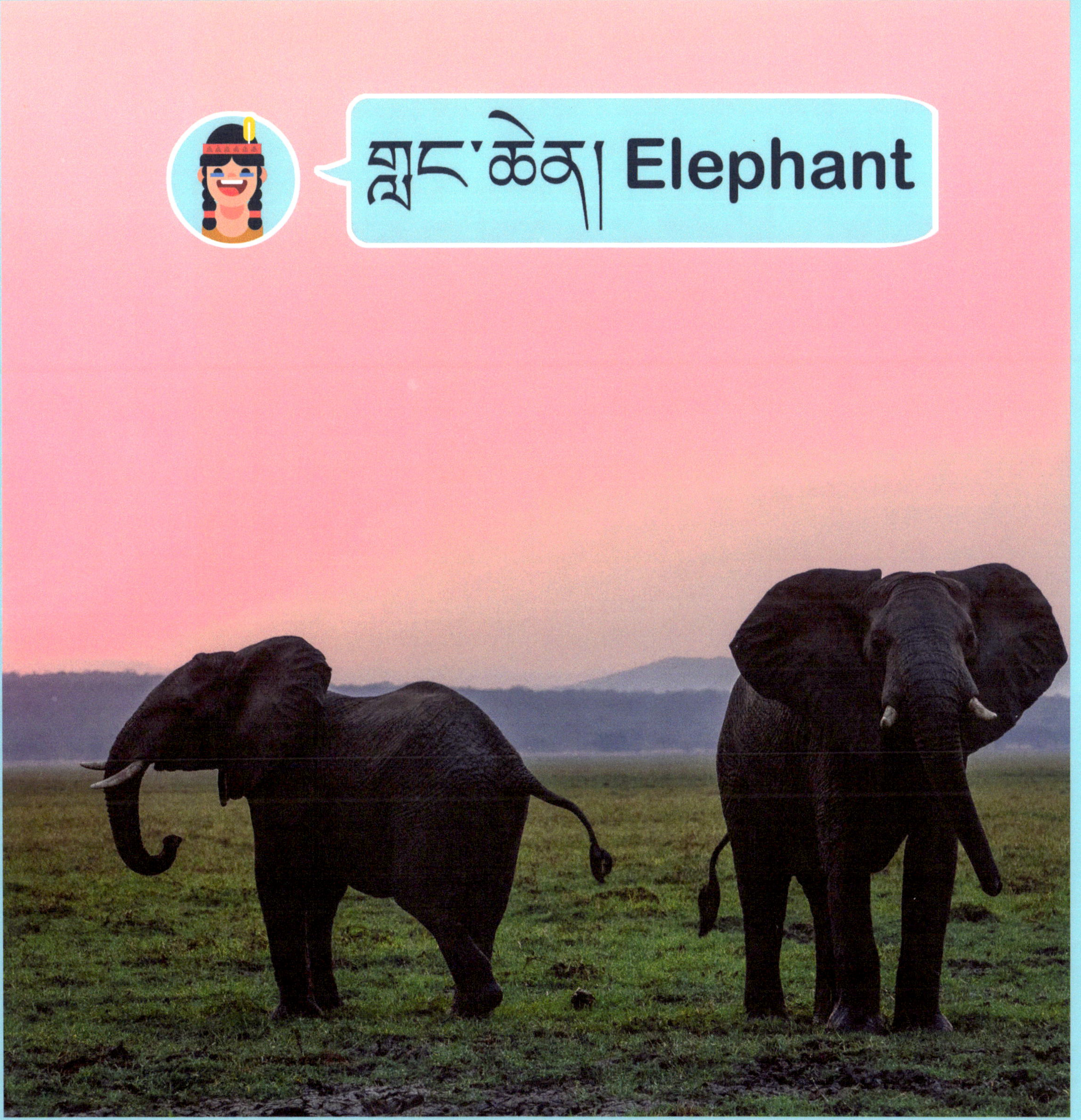

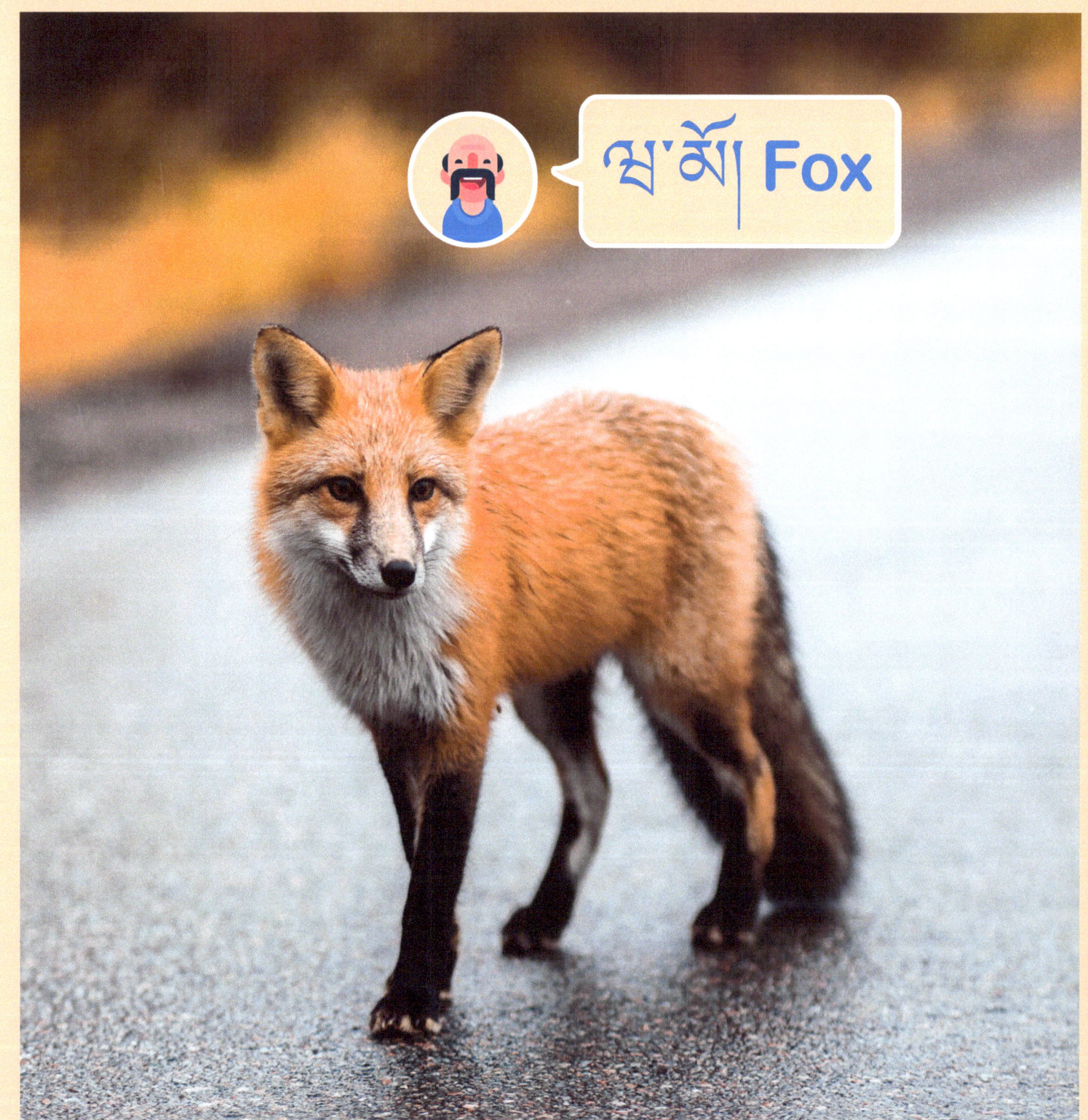

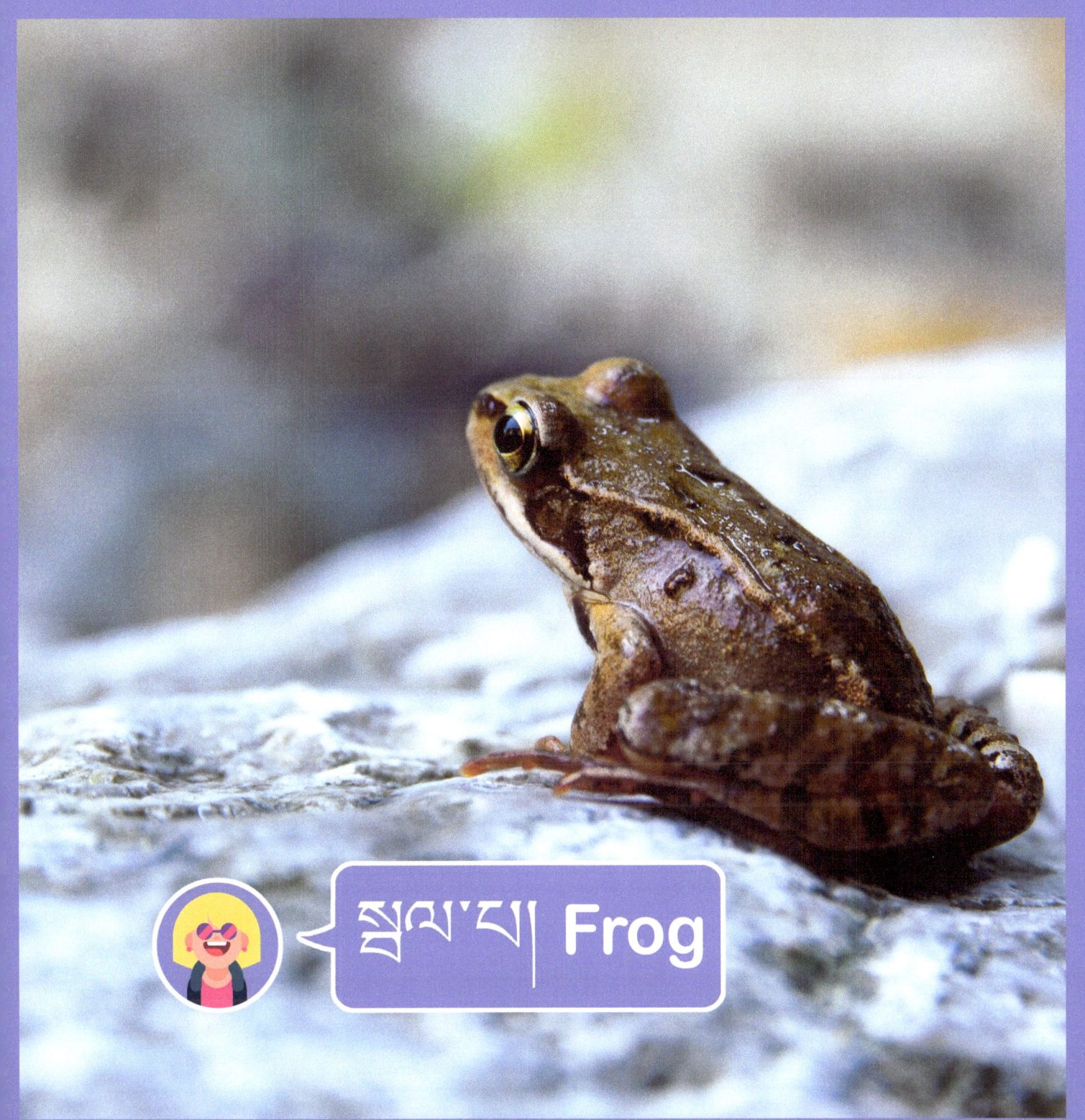

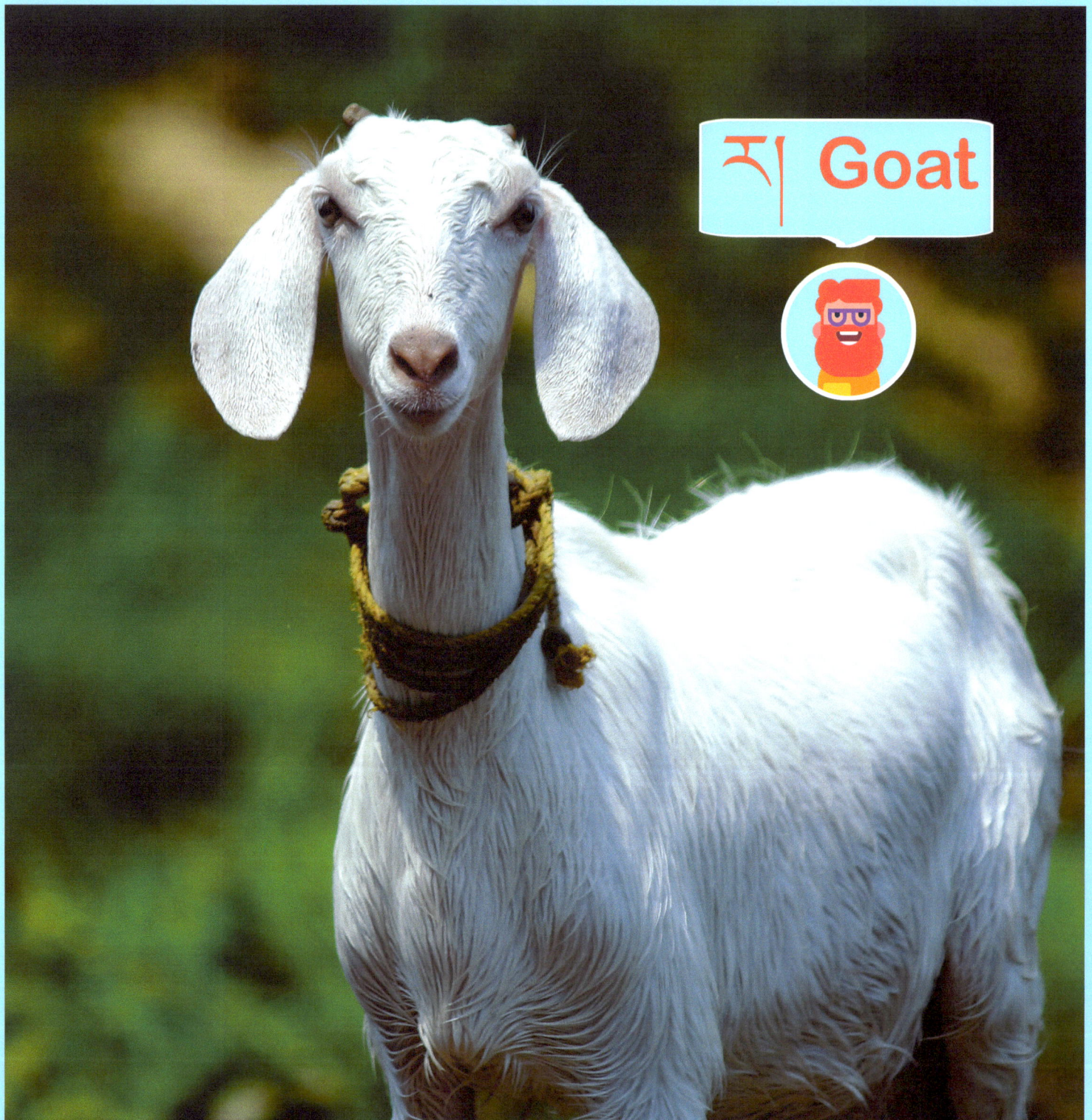

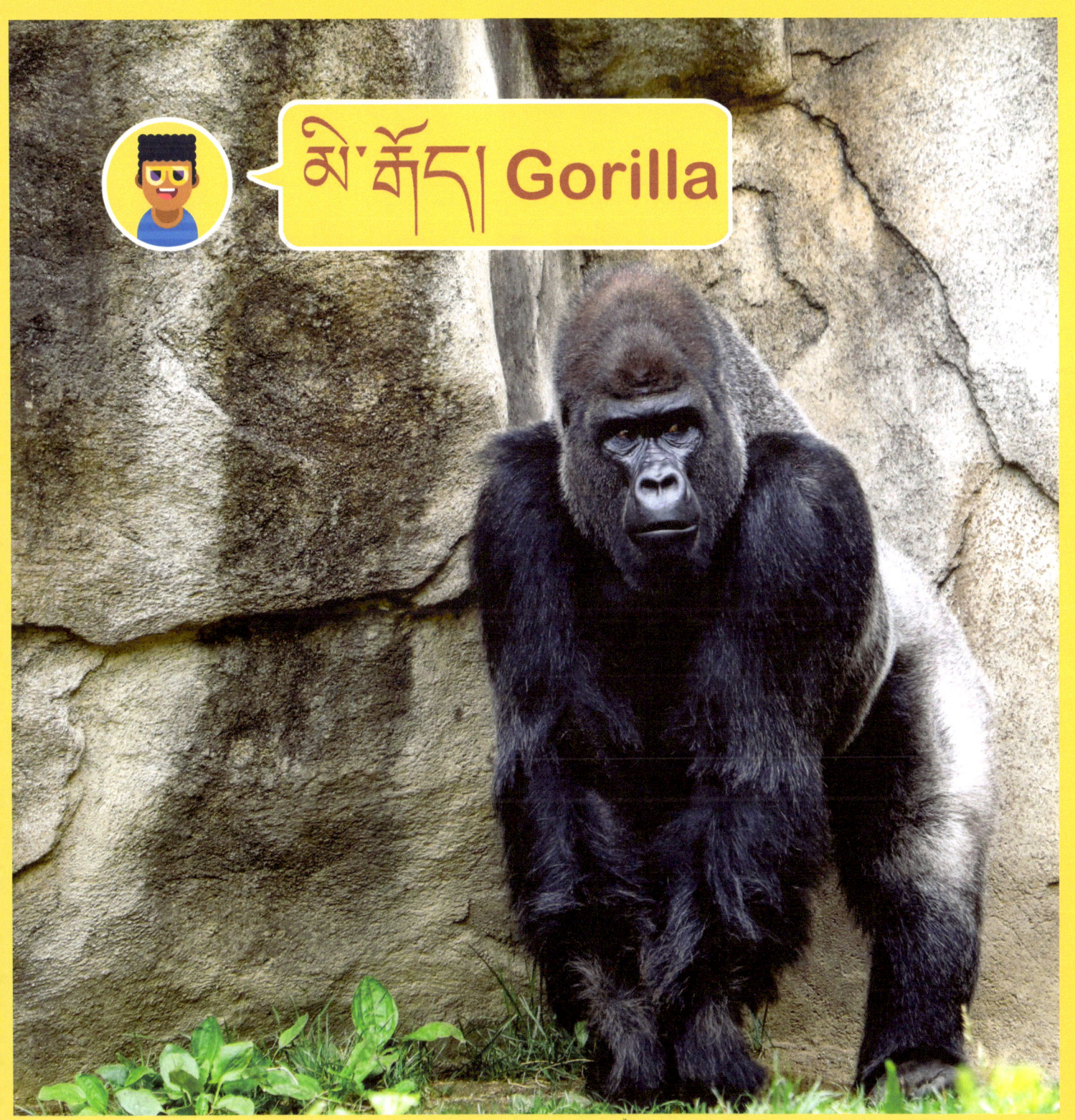

མི་ཚོད། Gorilla

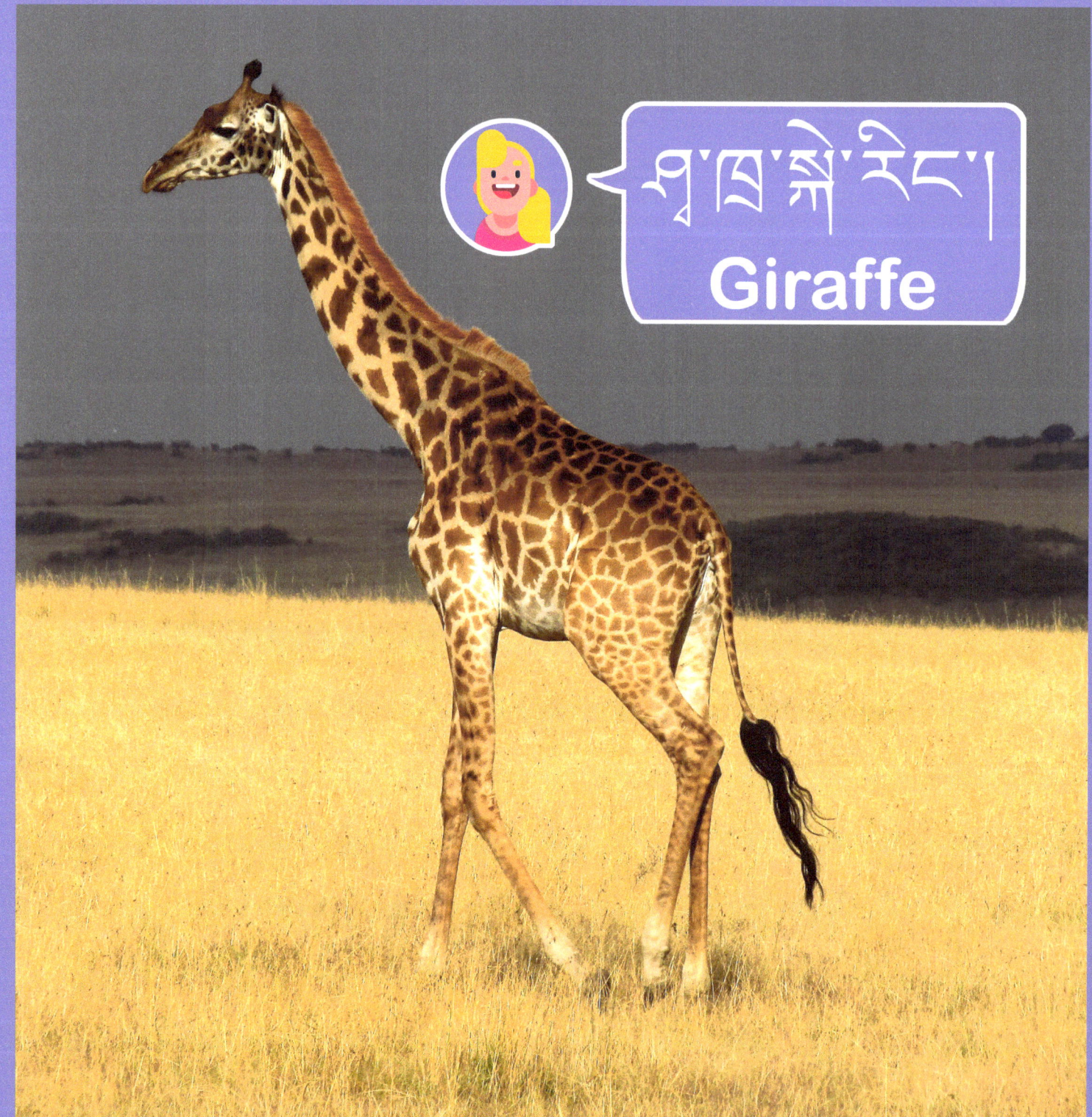

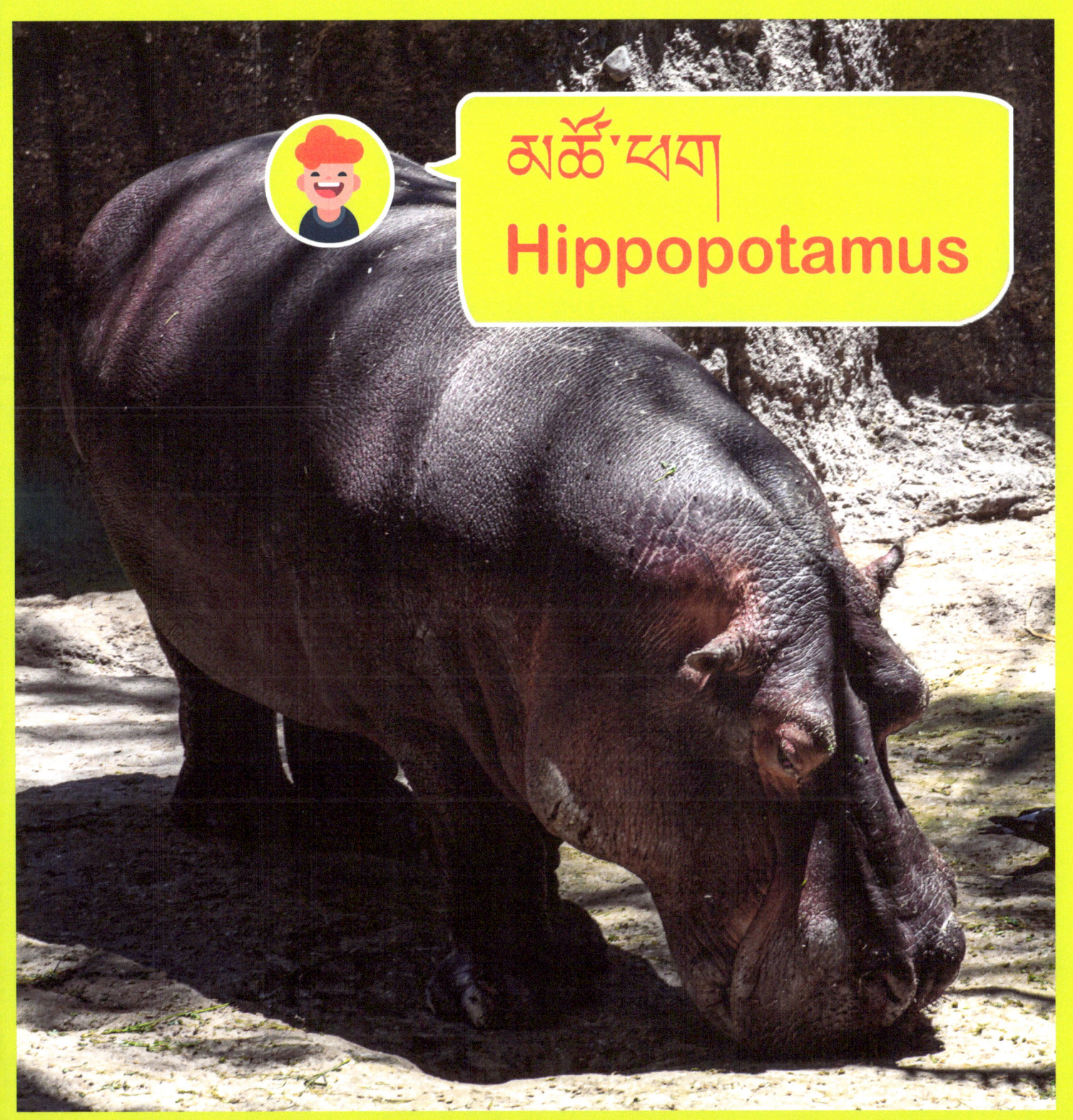

མཚོ་ཕག
Hippopotamus

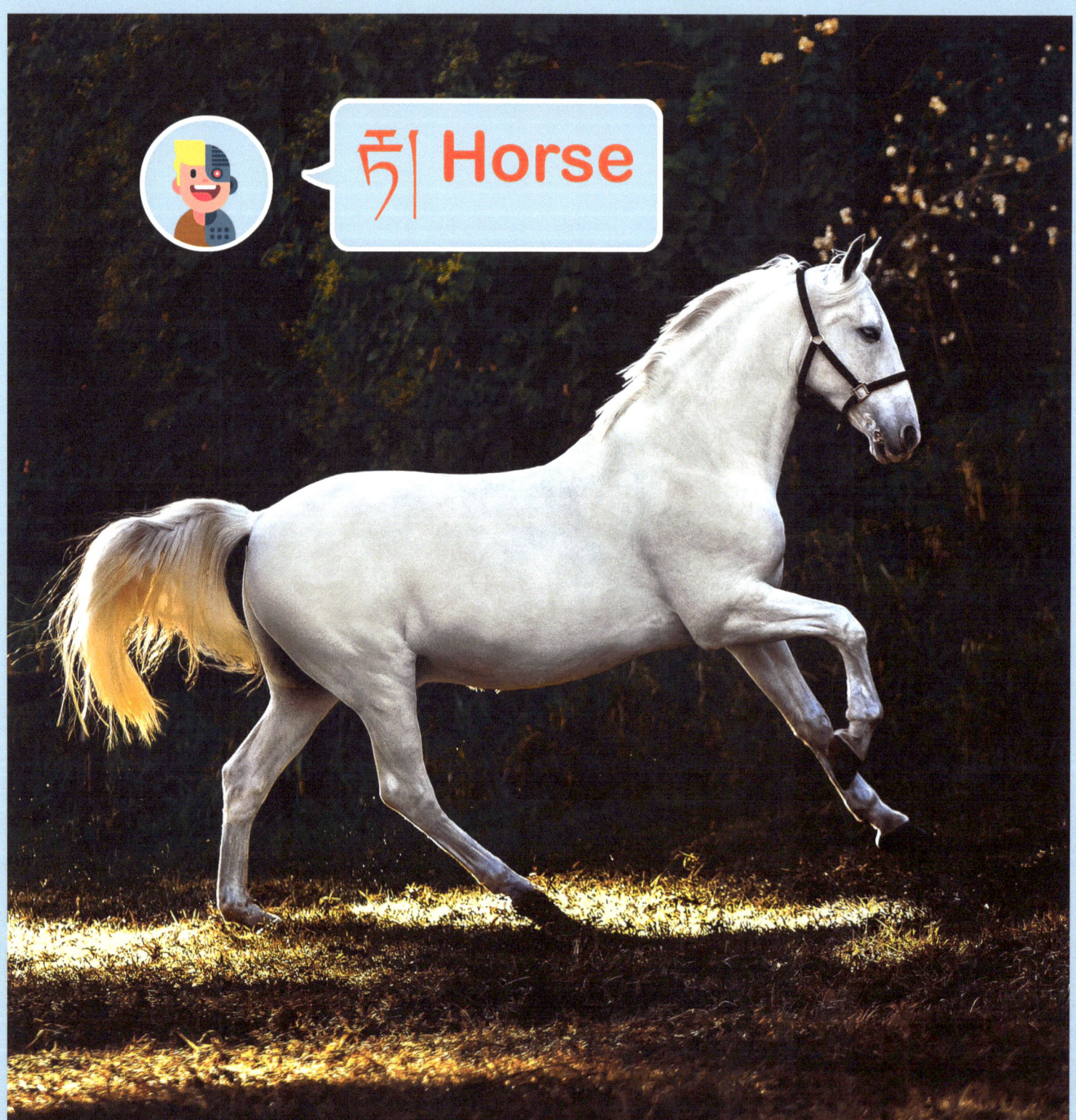

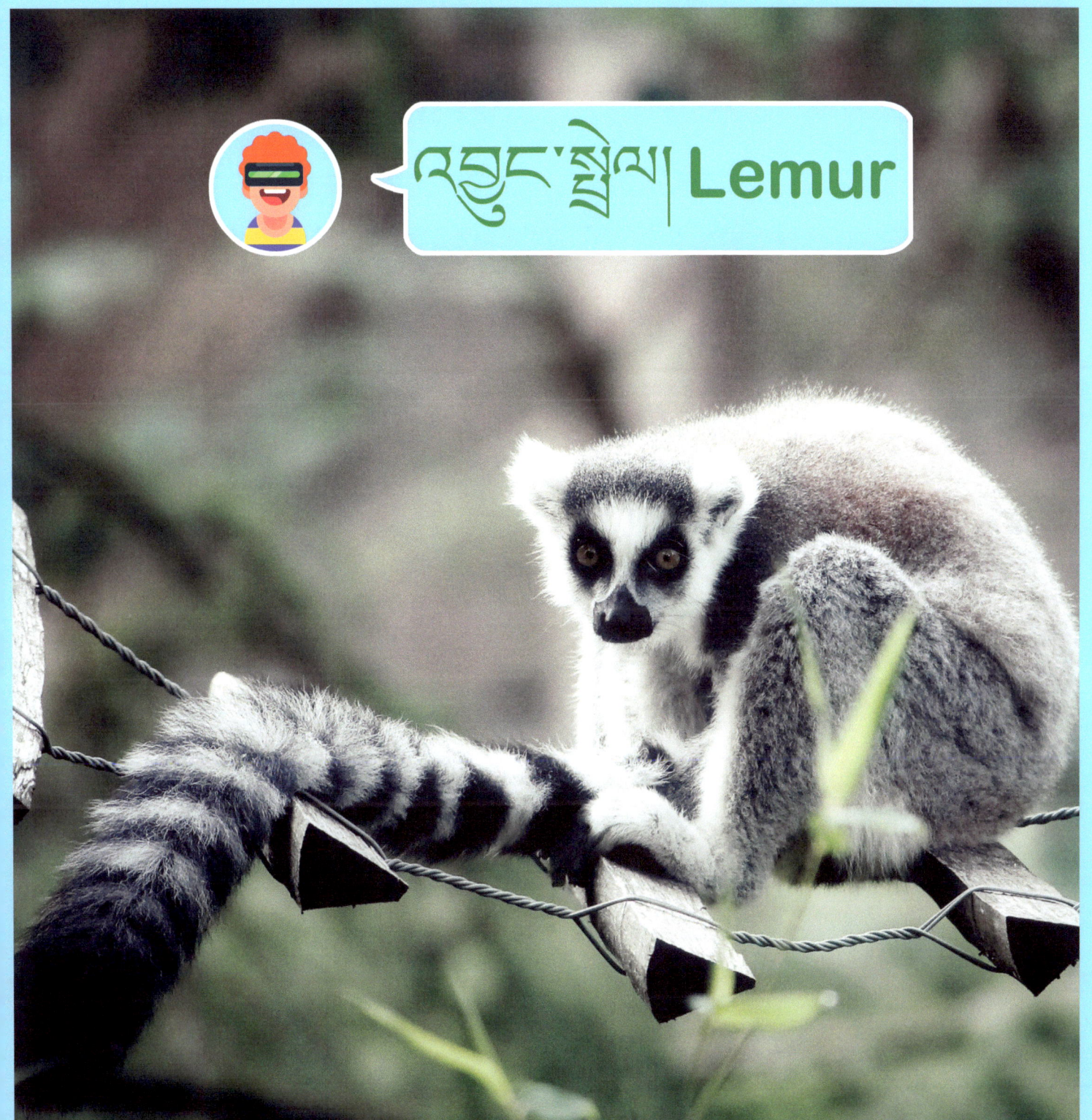

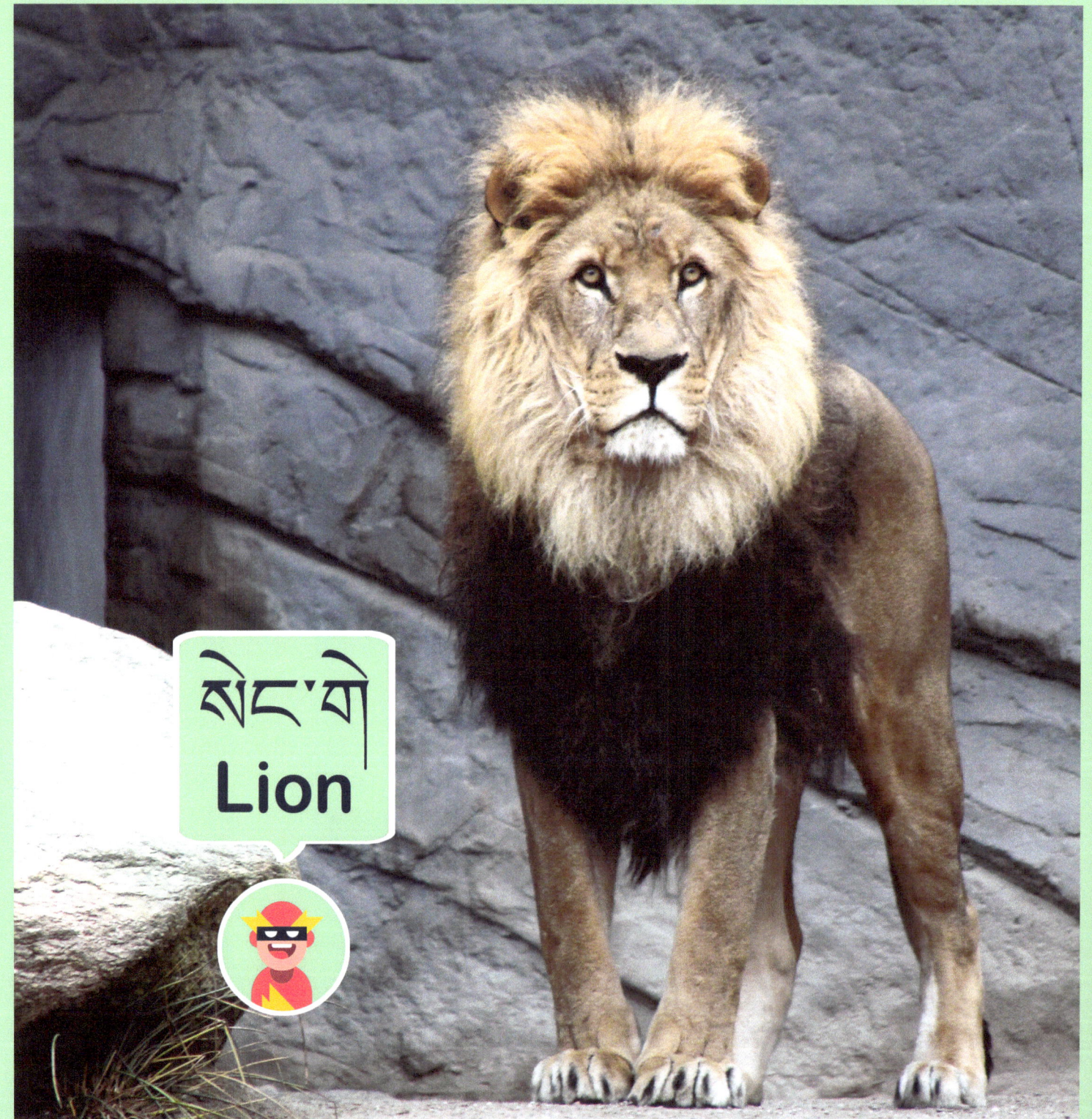

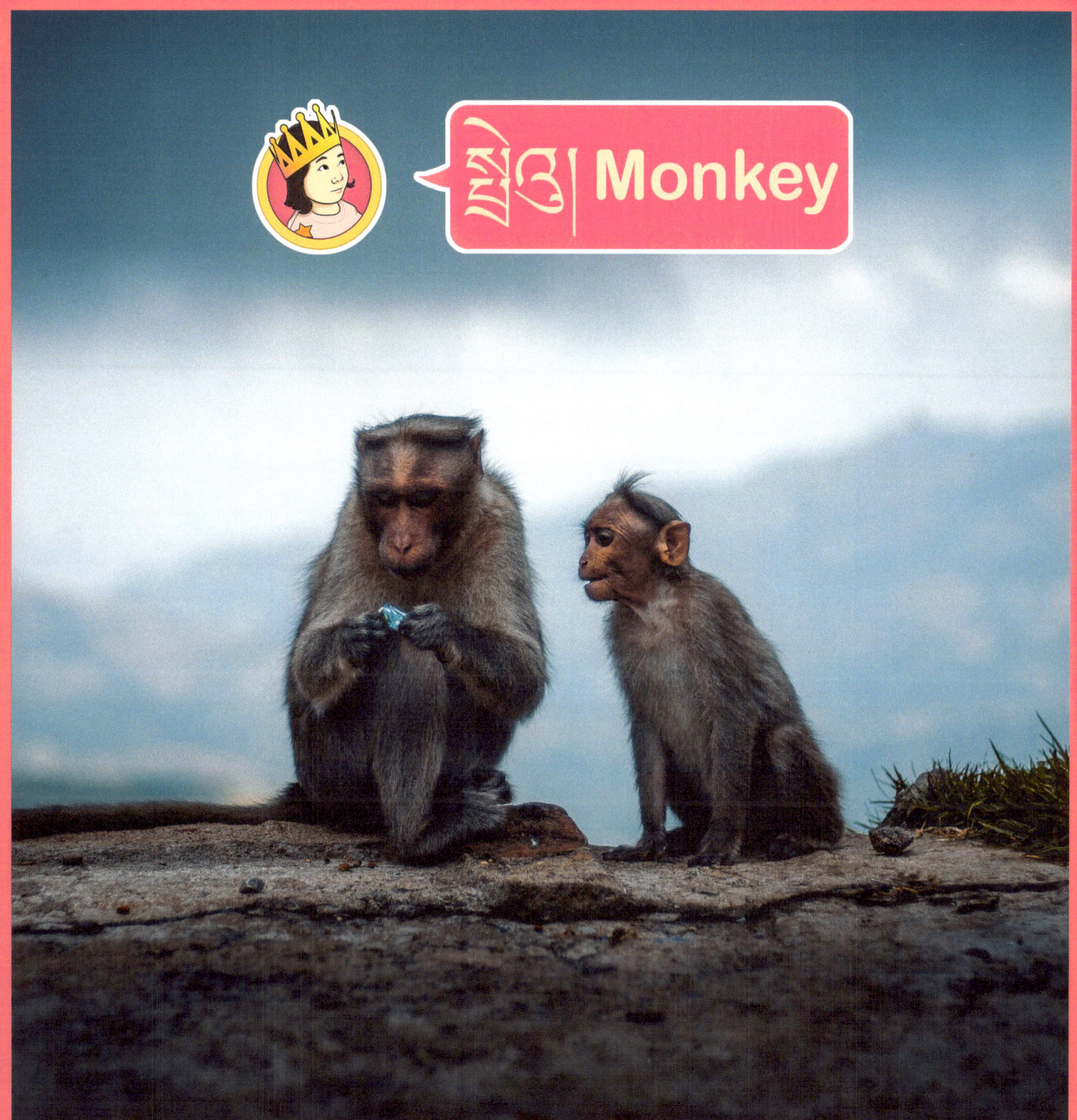

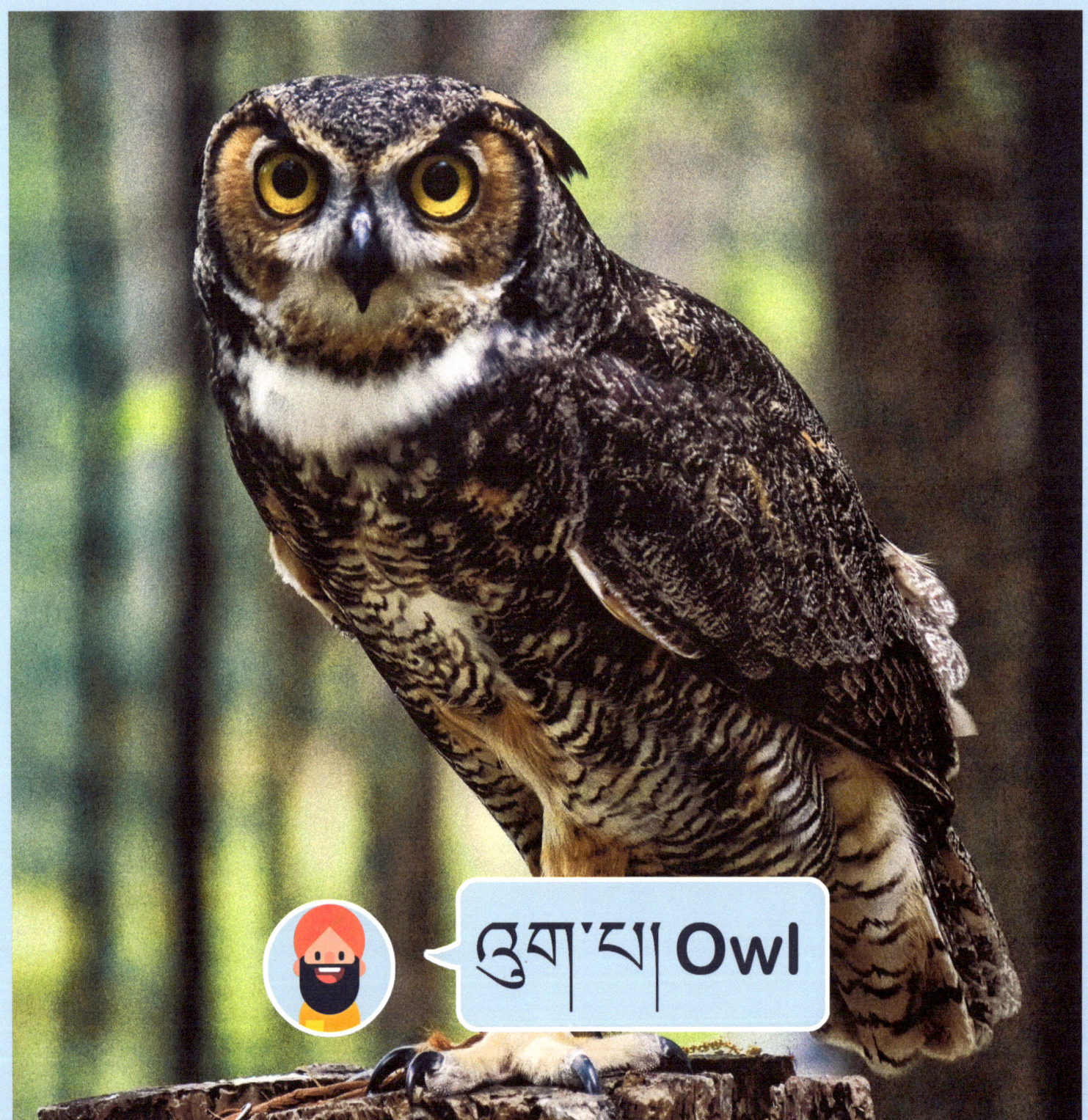

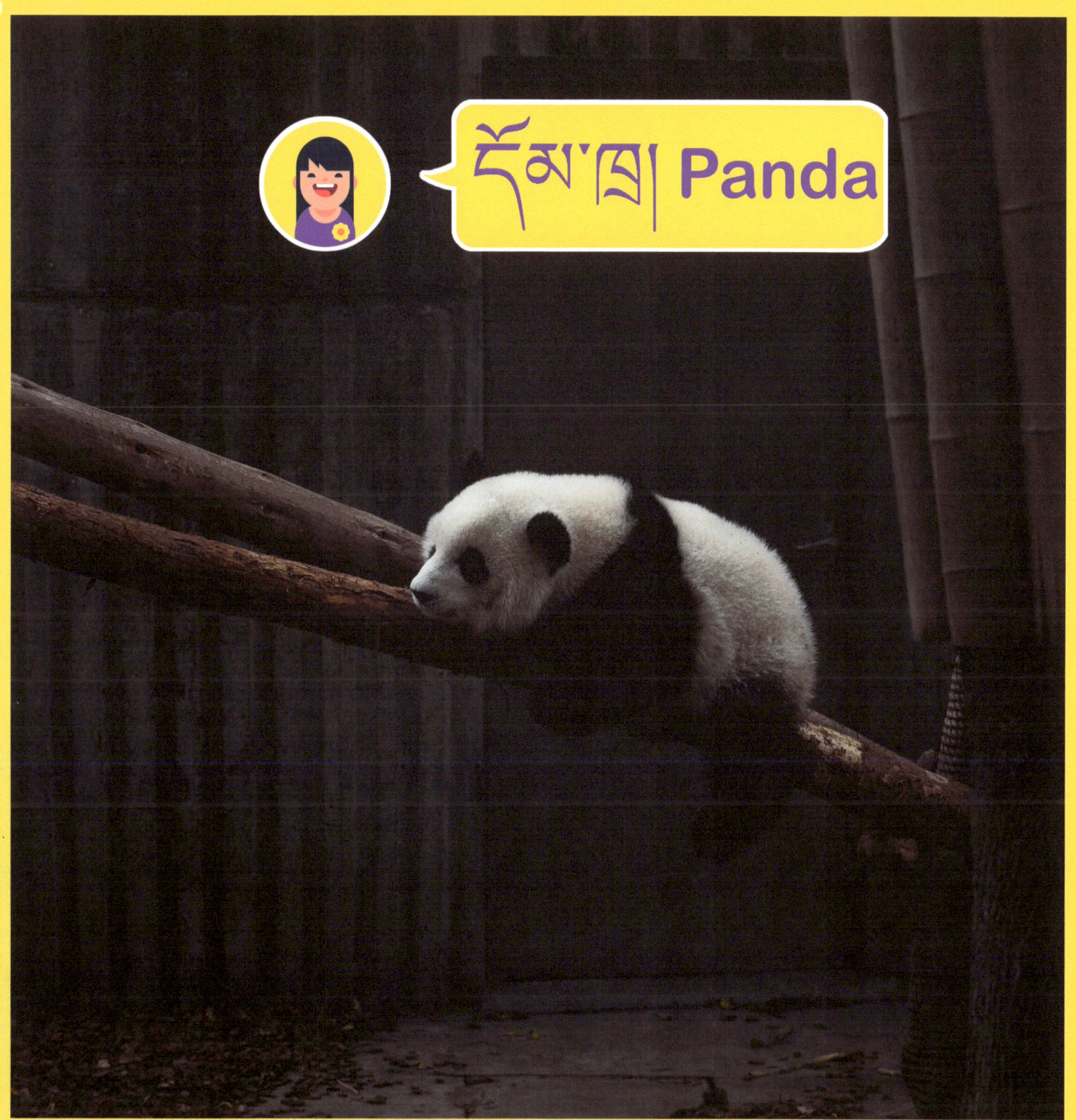

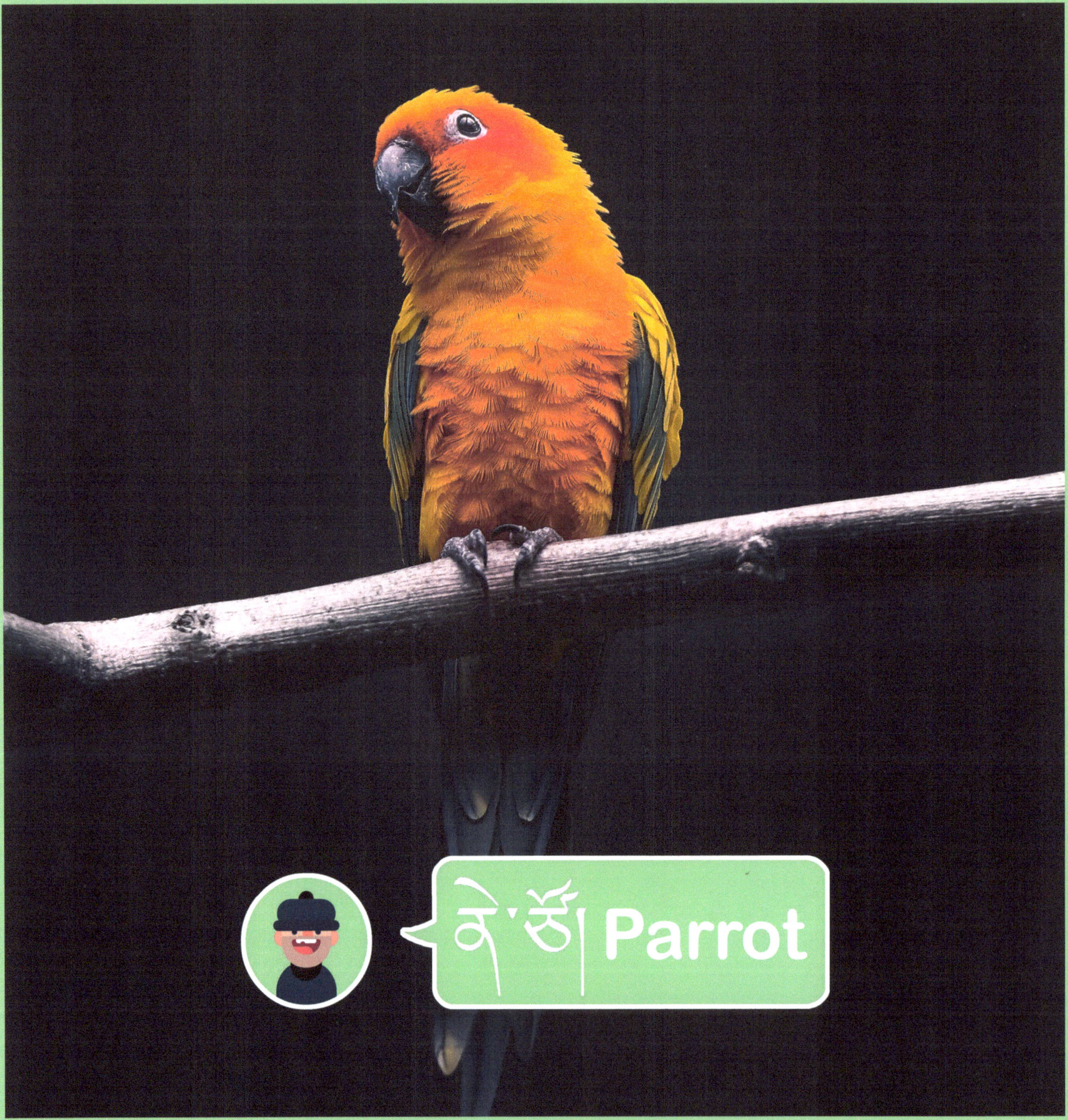

 ਕੇਂਕ Parrot

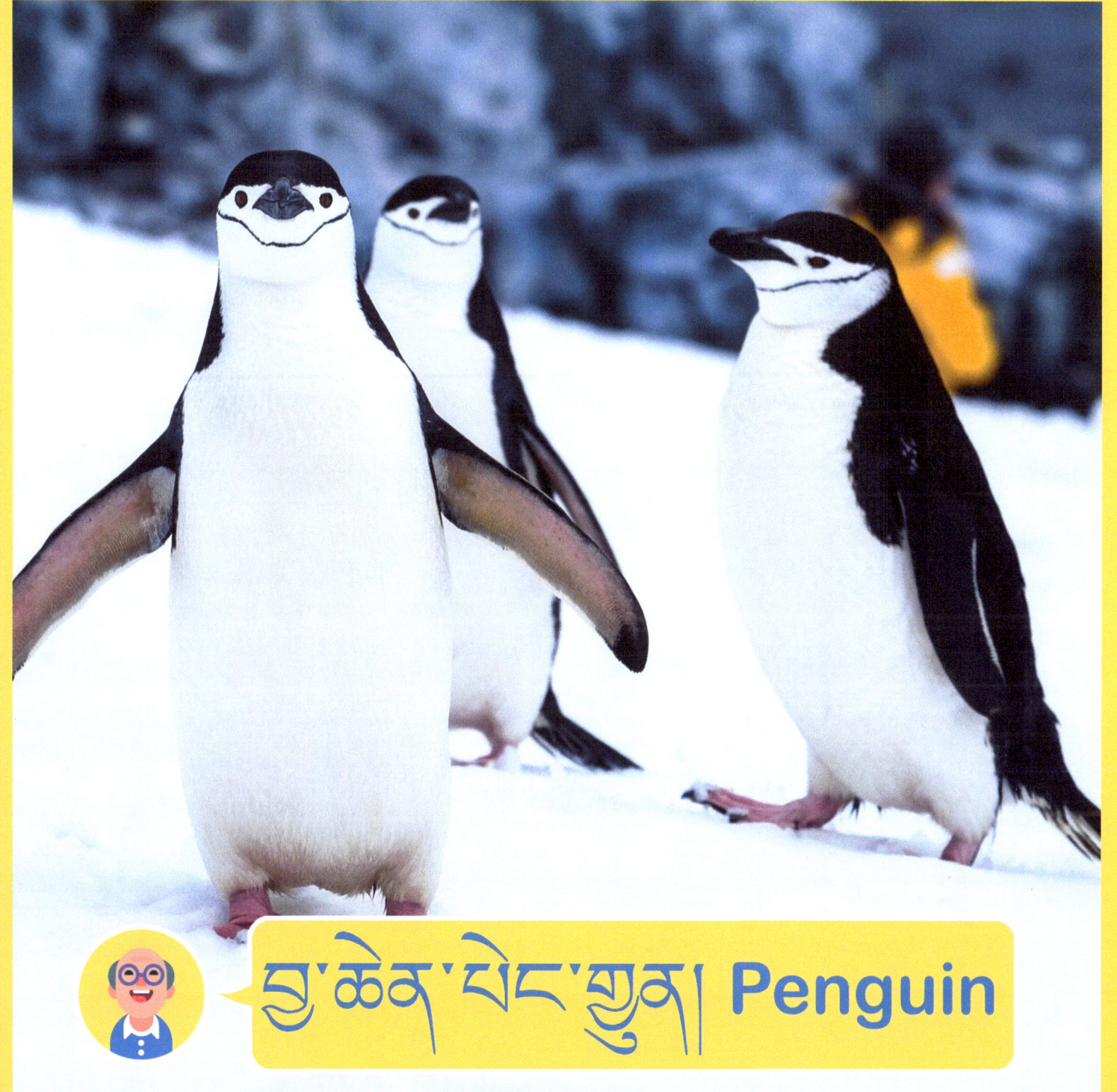

བྱུ་ཆེན་ཕེང་གུན། Penguin

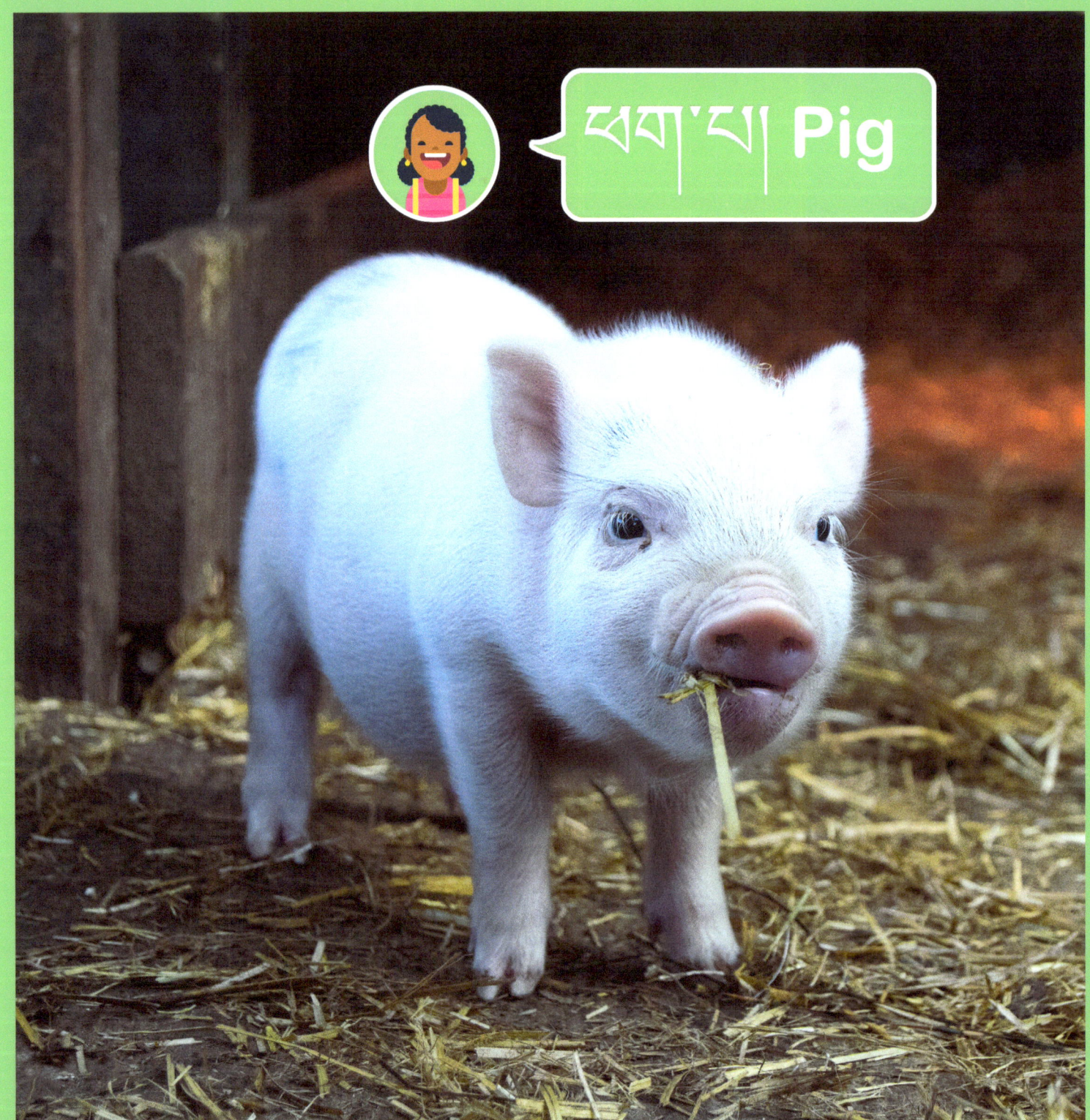

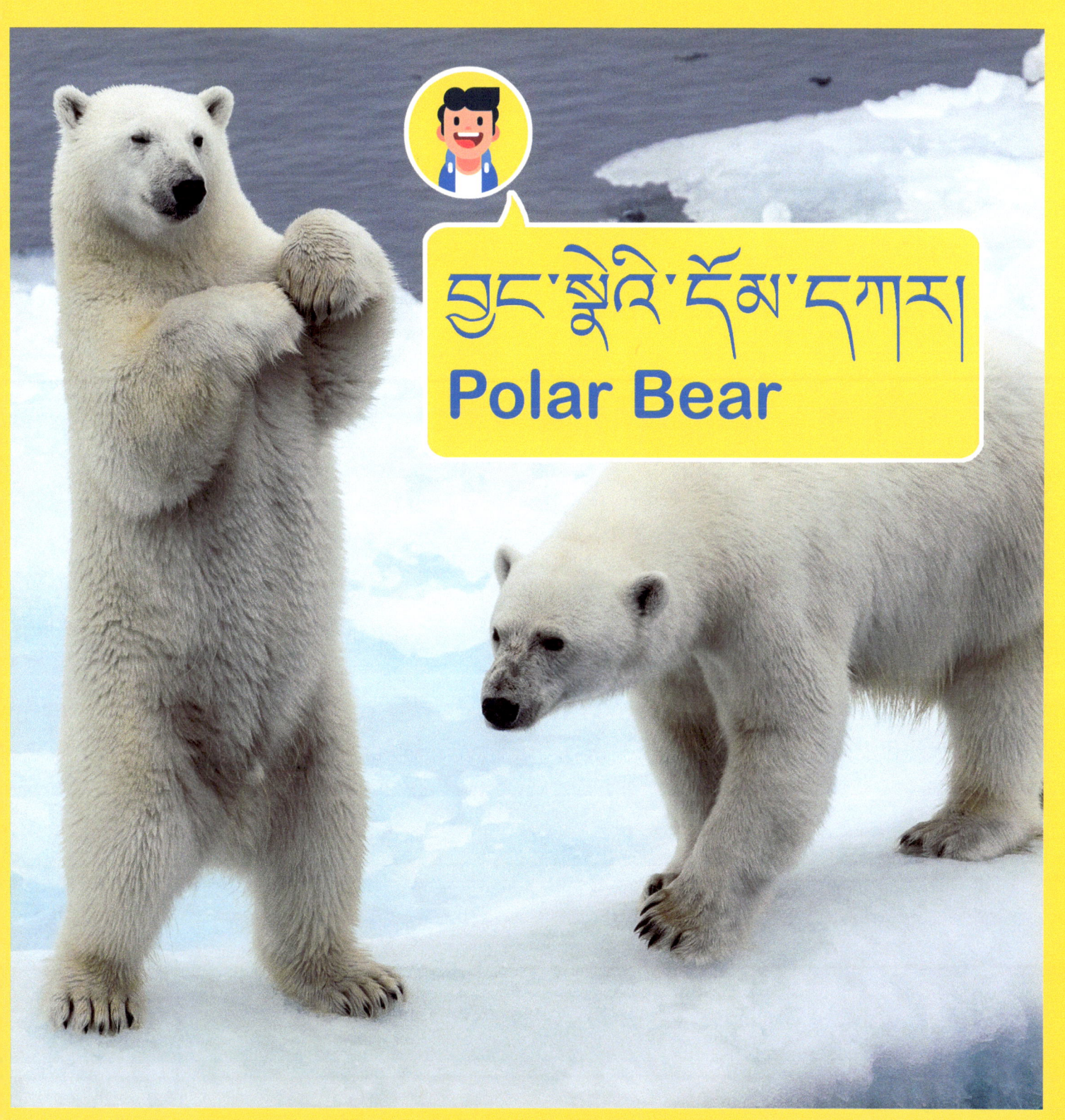

གྱང་སྐྱའི་དོམ་དཀར།
Polar Bear

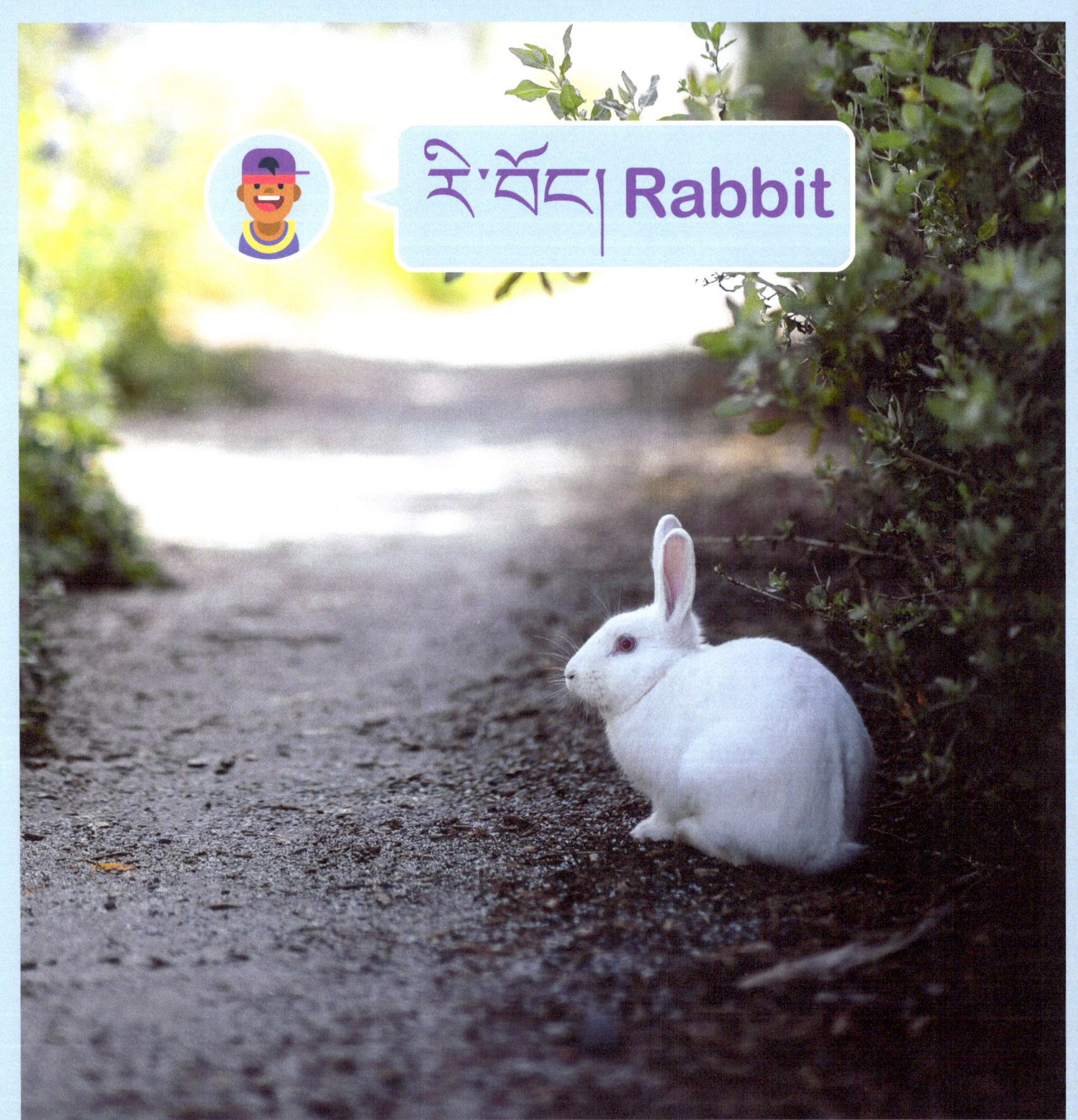

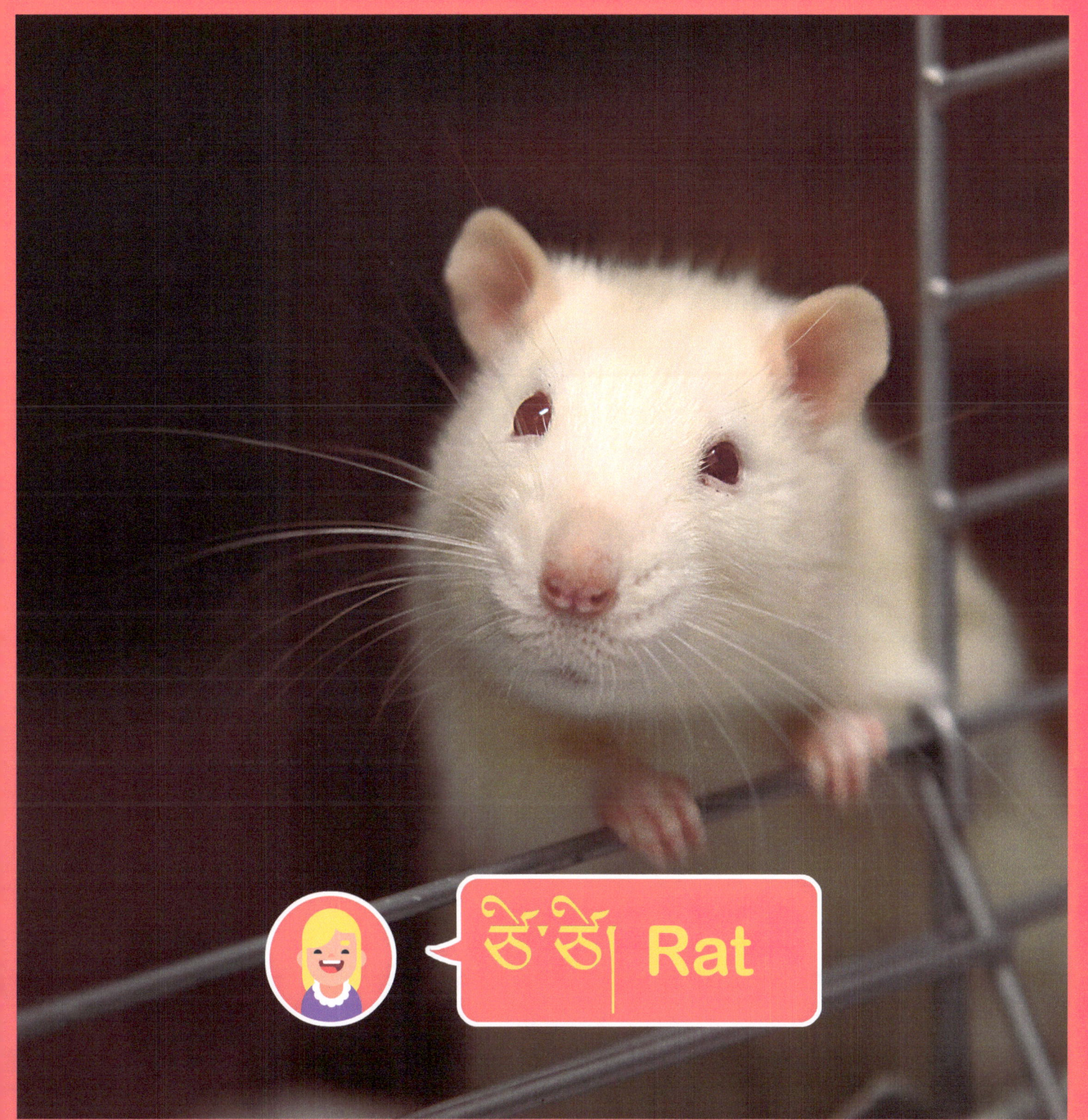

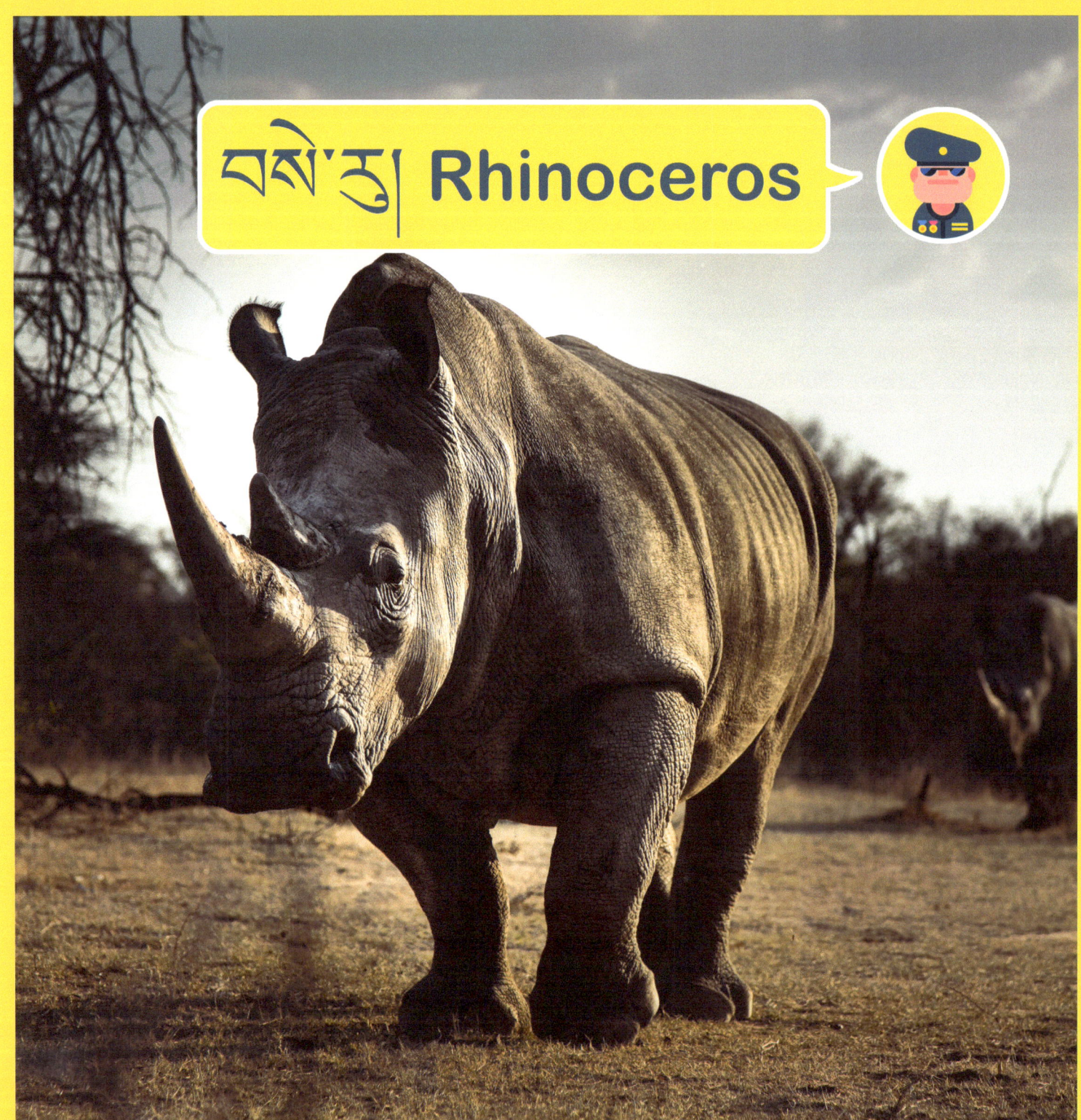

བསེ་རུ། Rhinoceros

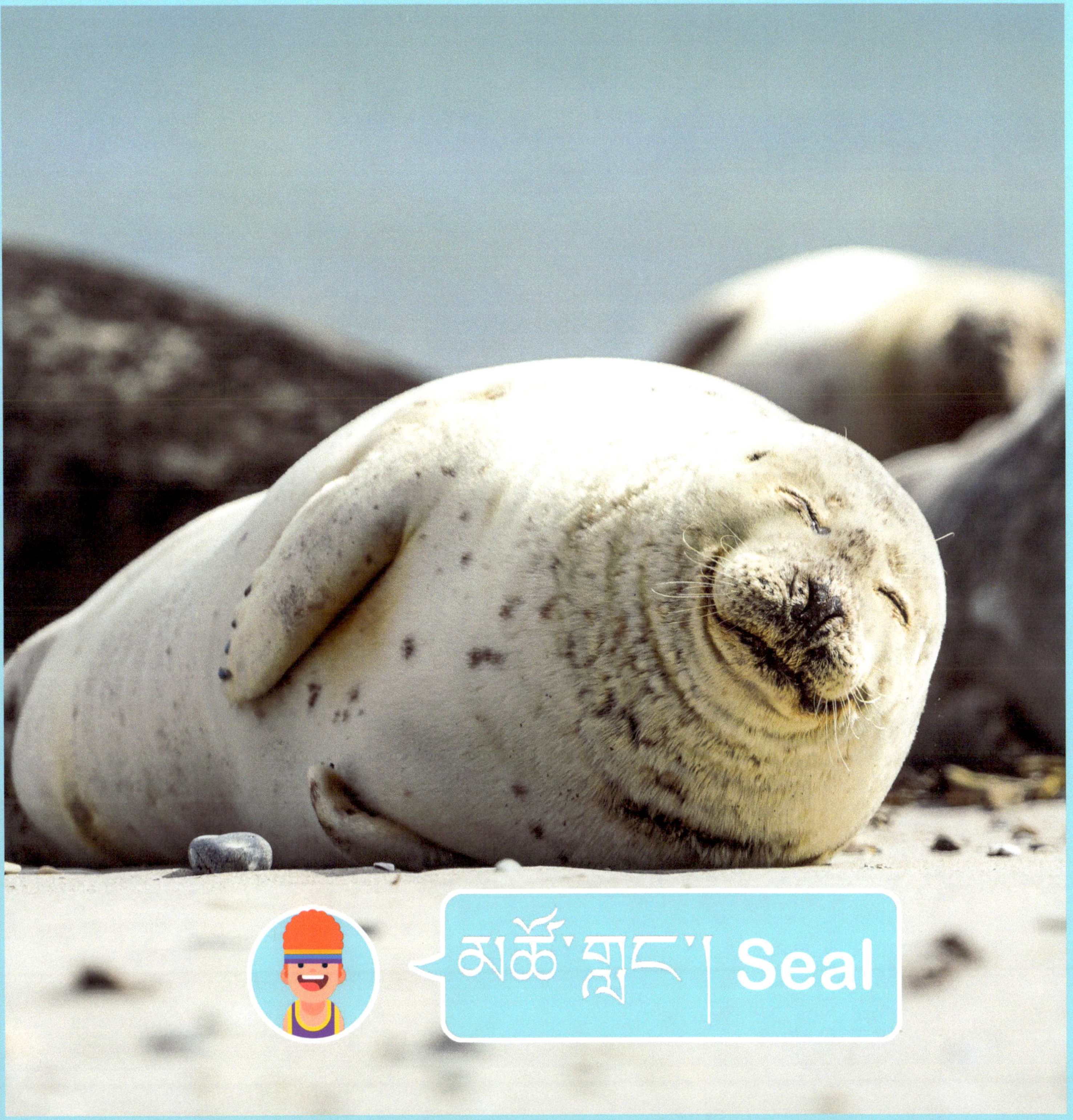

 མཚོ་སྦྲང་། Seal

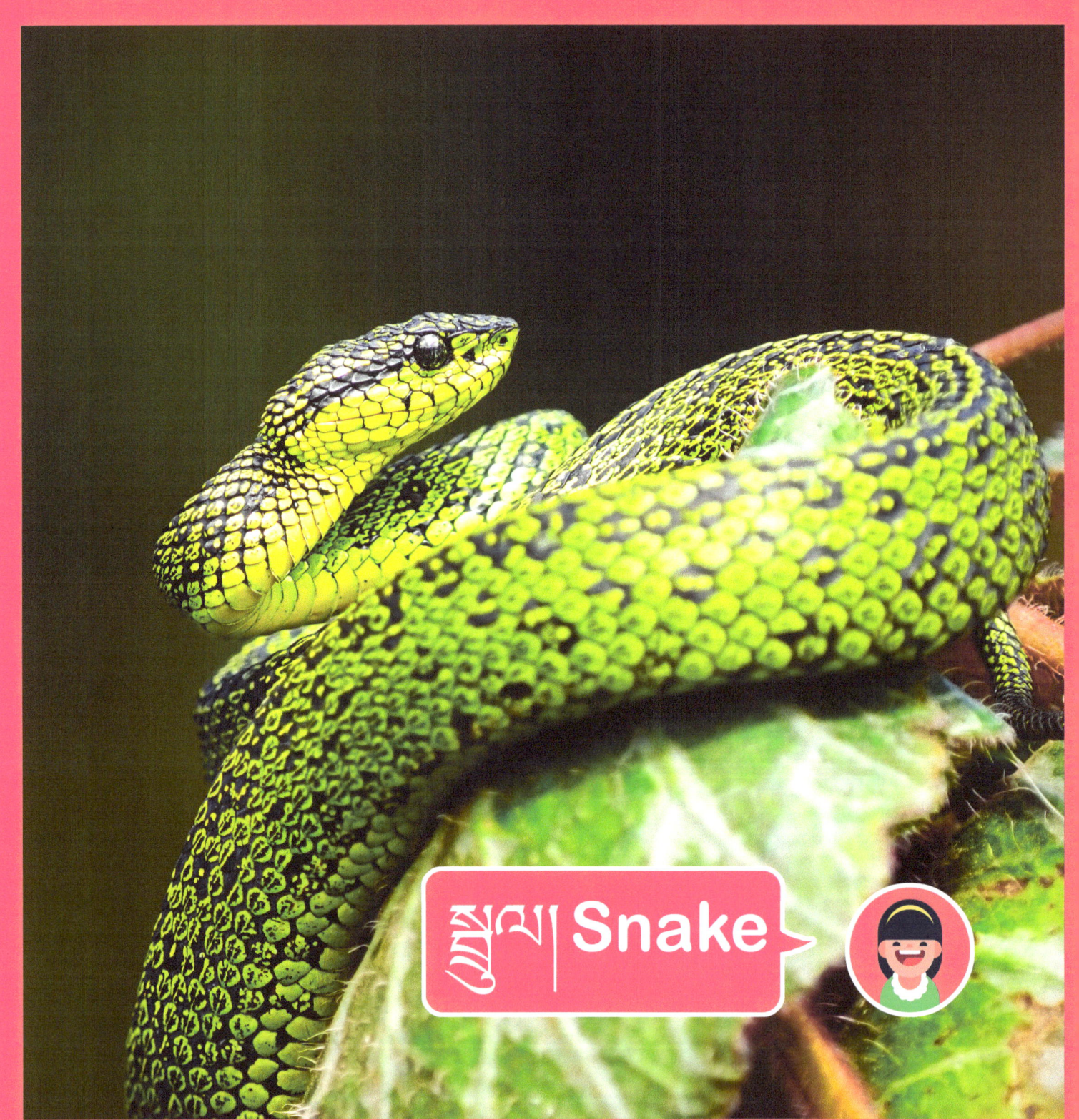

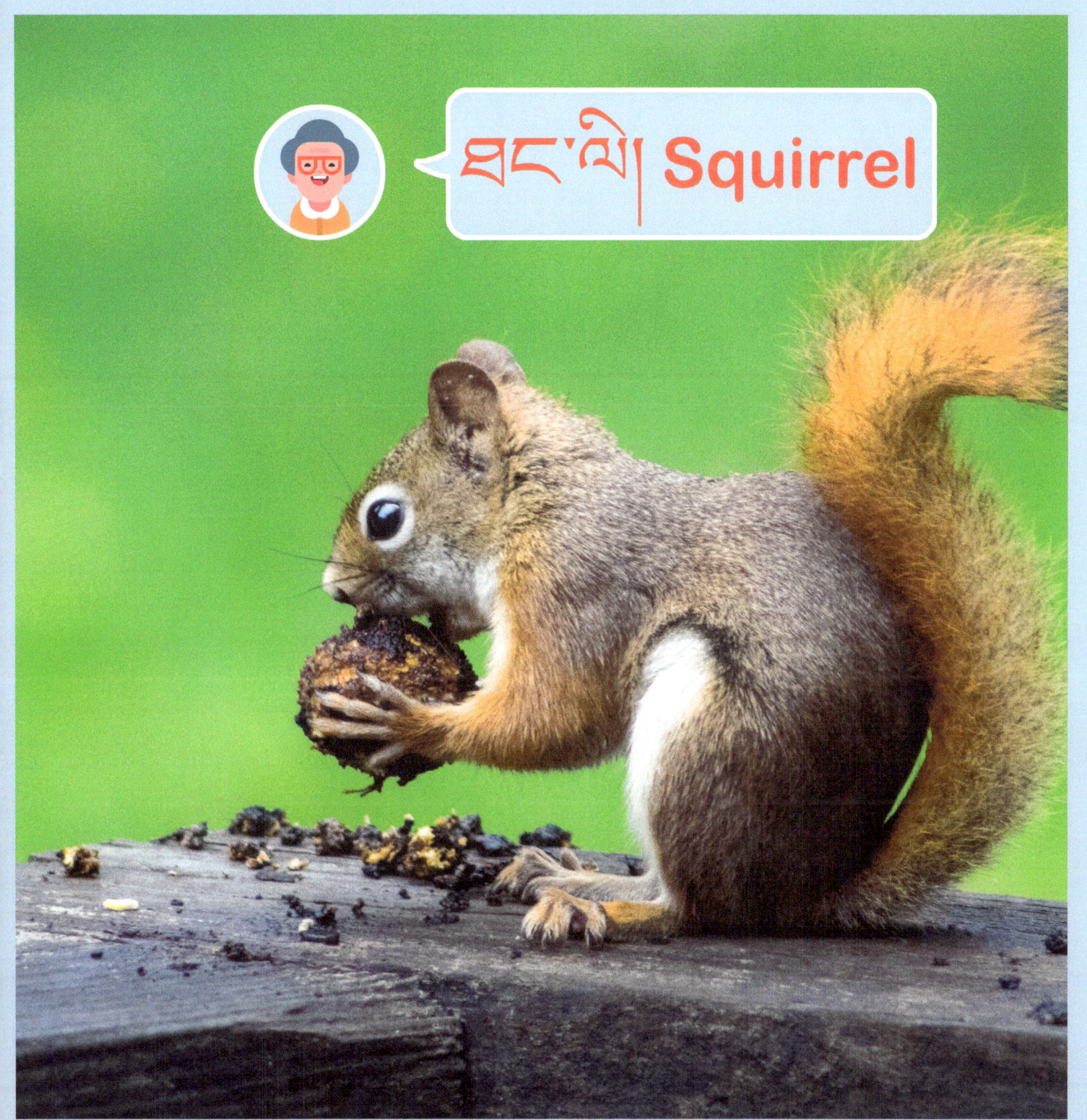

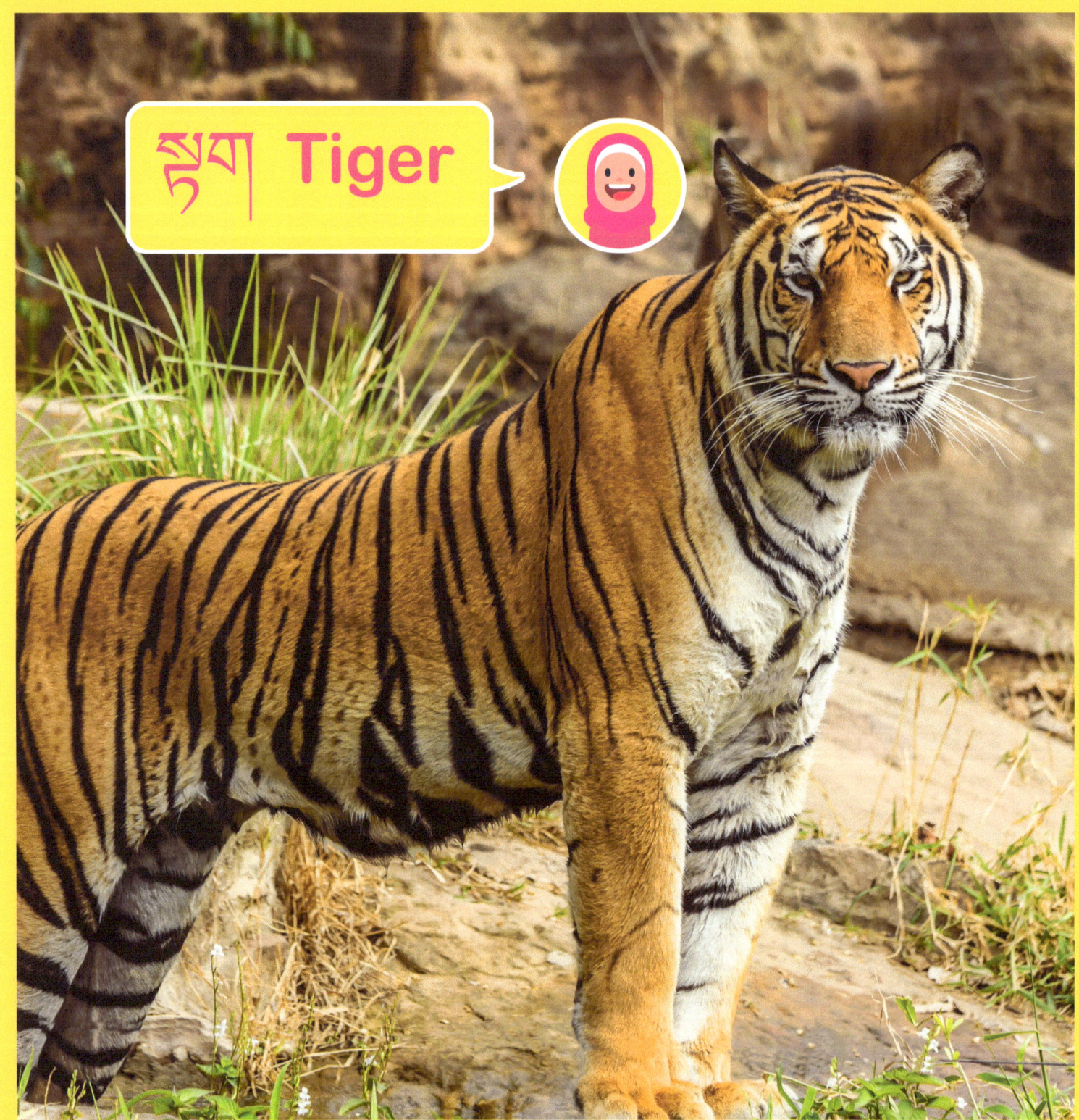

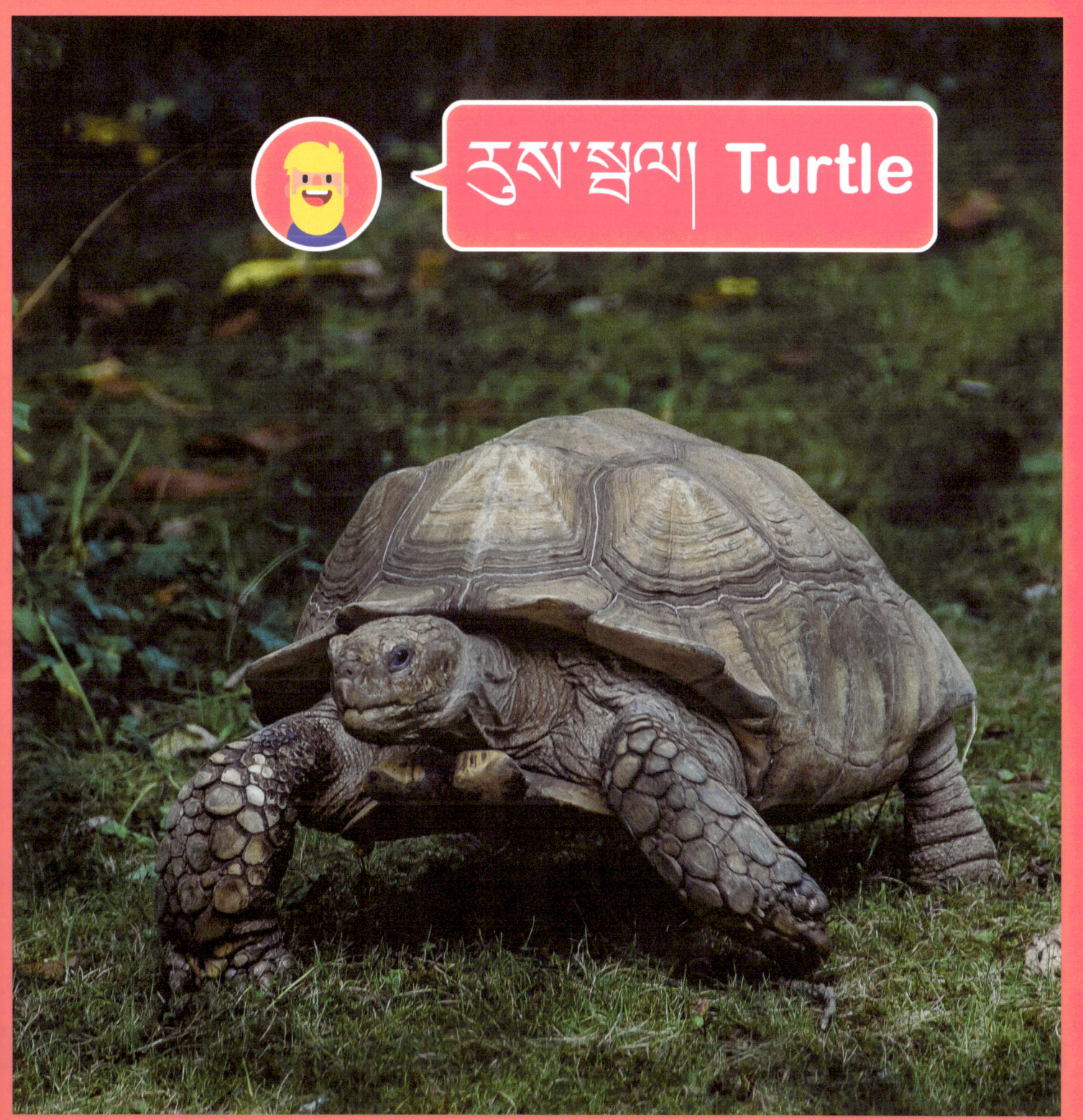

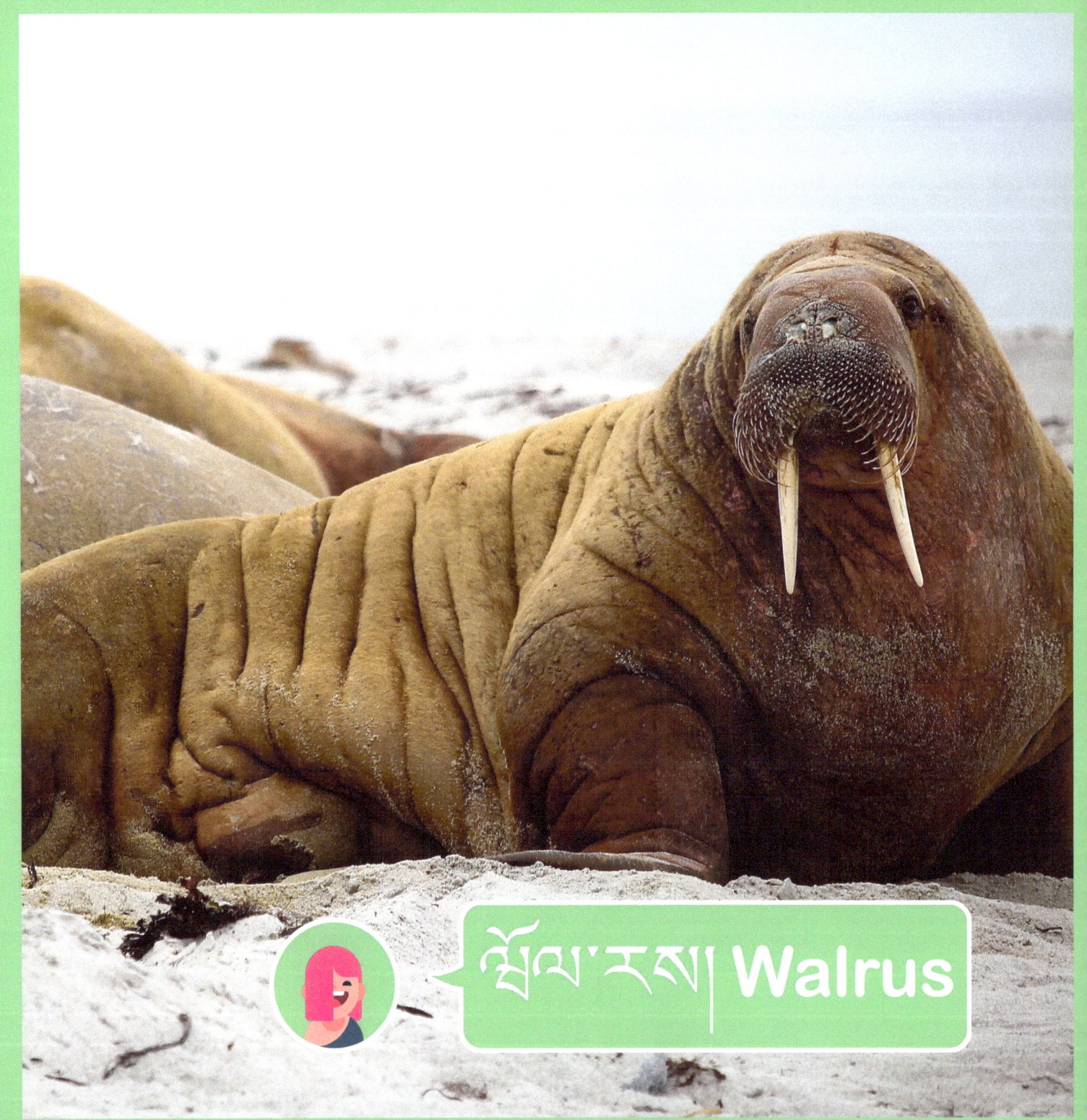

བྱོལ་རས། Walrus

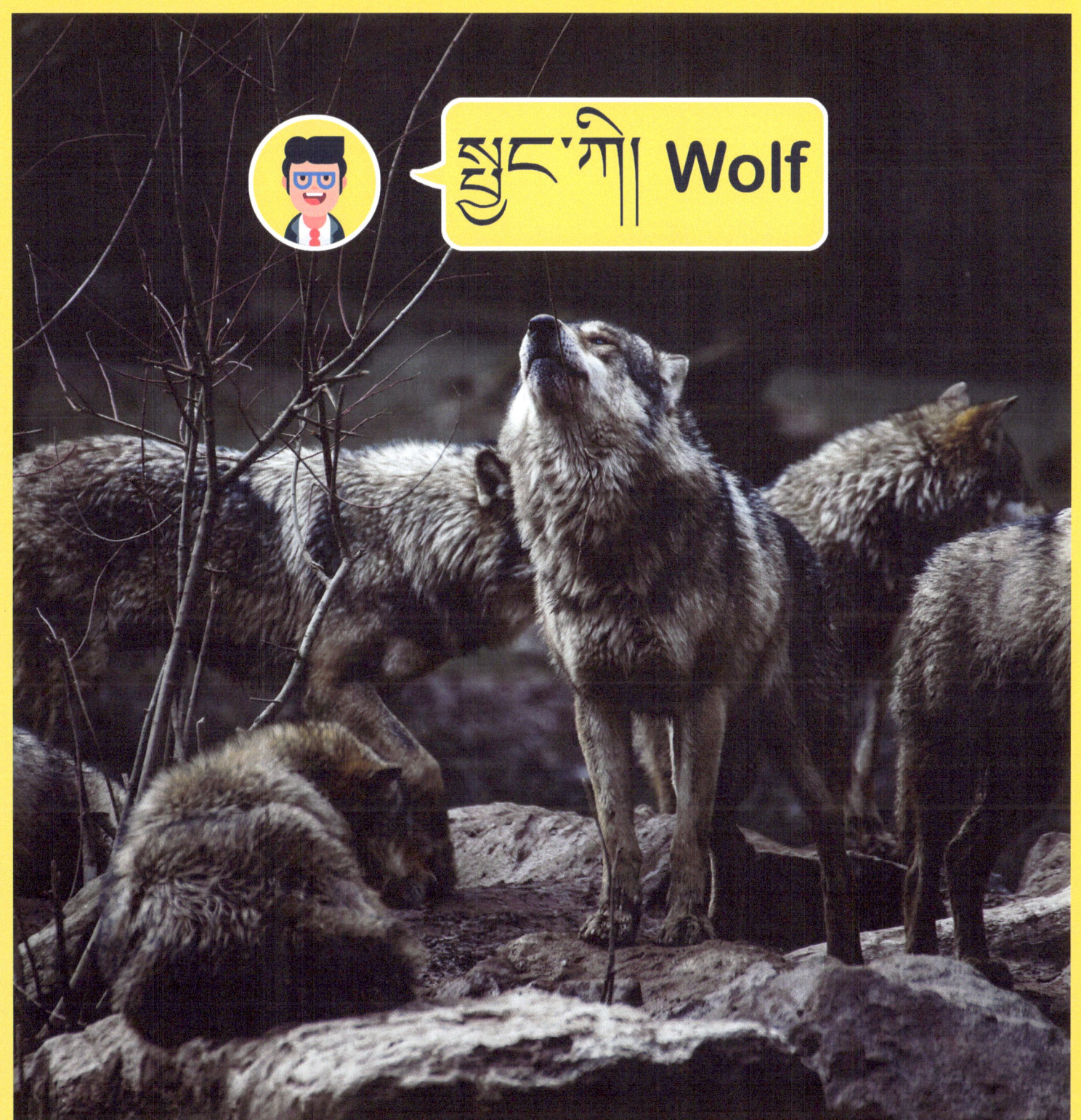

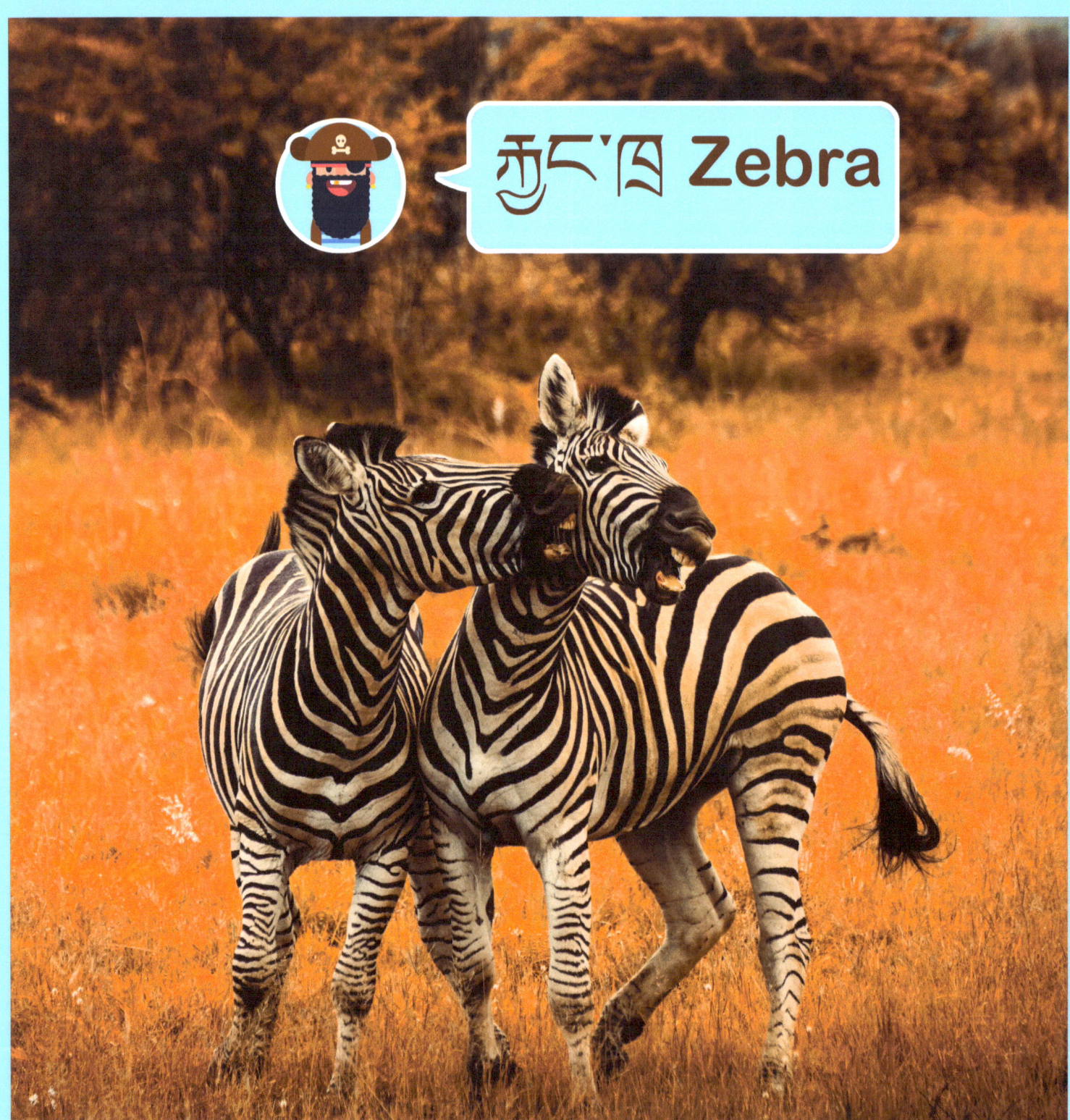

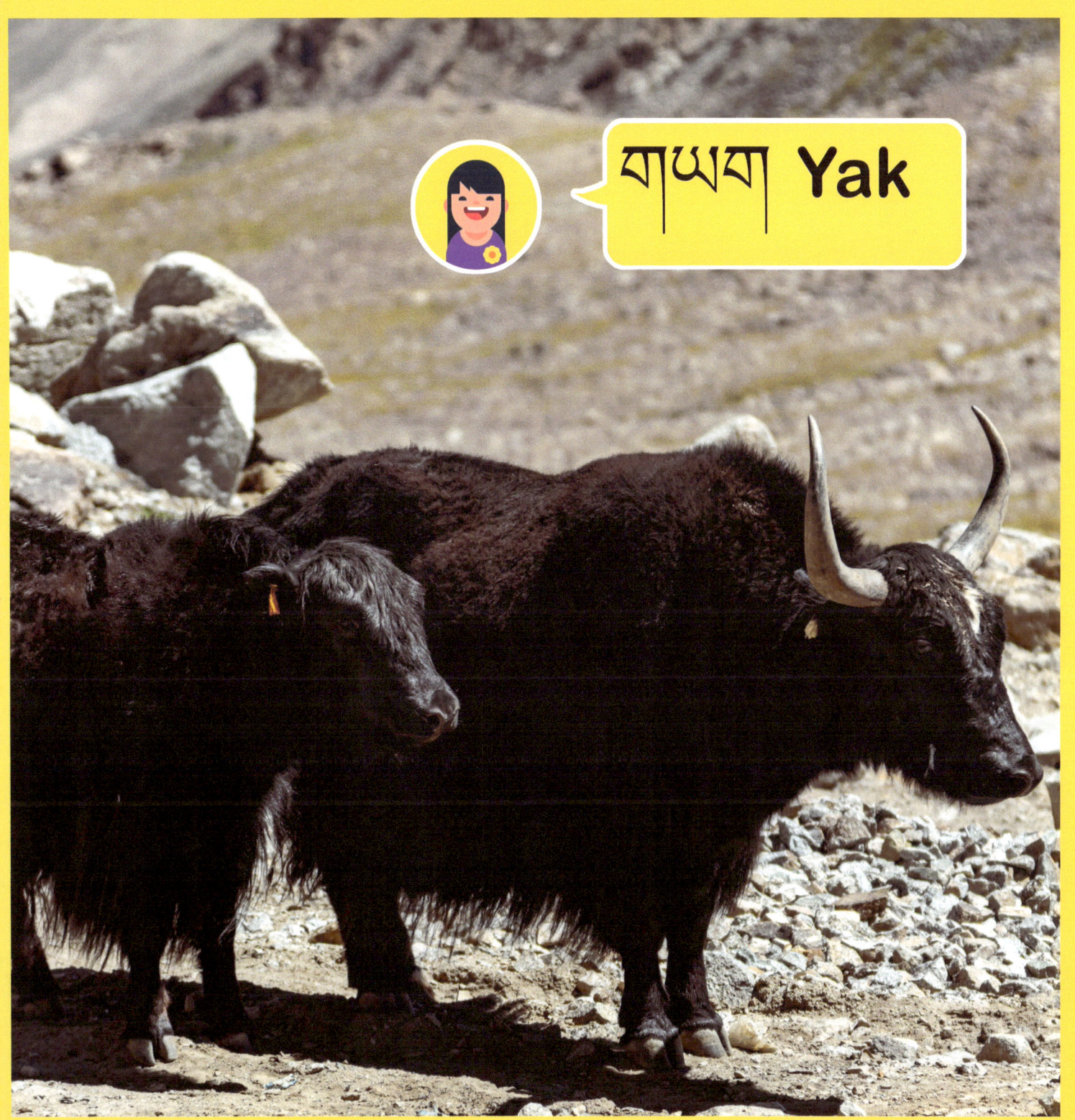

If you like this book, please leave a review and check out other Pema Play books available on Amazon.com

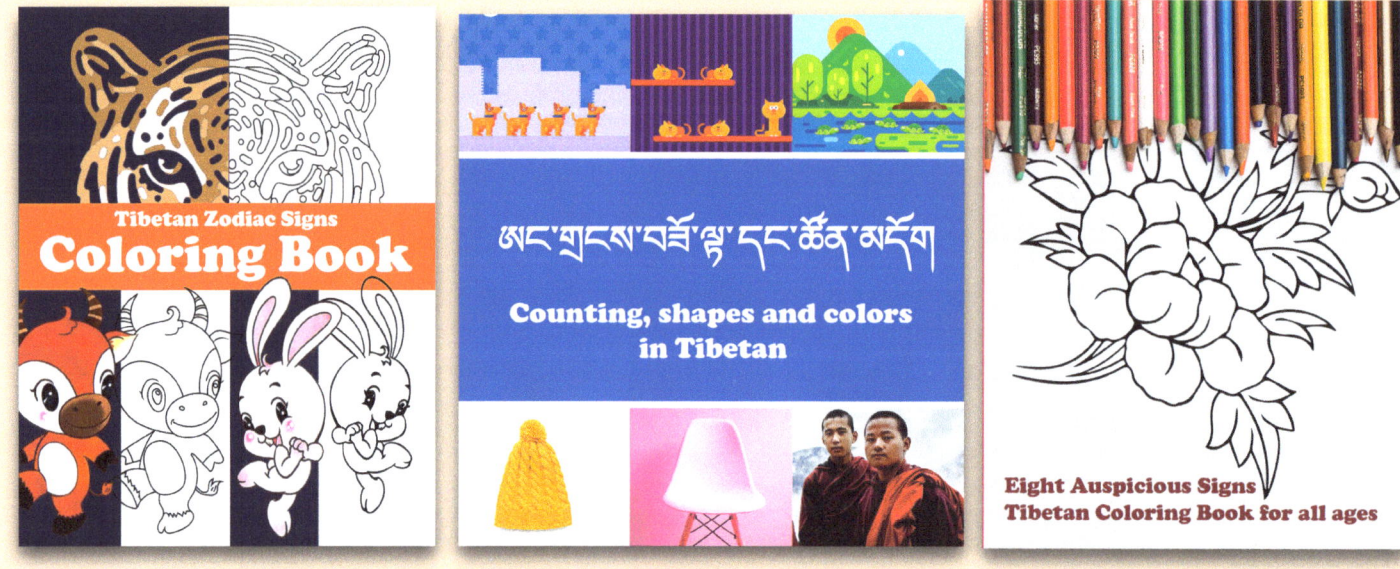

Thanks to Tenzin Norphel

Thanks to our image contributors: A G, Ahmed Zayan, Alexander London, Alfonso Castro, Amy Reed, Angel Luciano, Ansgar Scheffold, Brian McMahon, Caleb Martin, Christopher Carson, Crisoforo Gaspar Hernandez, Derek Oyen, Erik Mclean, Erik-Jan Leusink, Helena Lopes, Jason Leung, Jay Ruzesky, Keith Markilie, Kevin Mueller, Laura College, Luca Ambrosi, Mathew Schwartz, Mika Brandt, Mona Jain, Mylon Ollila, Nandhu Kumar, Ningyu He, Pascal Mauerhofer, Piera riva, prince patel, redcharlie, Samuel Giacomelli, Screenroad, Sonder Quest, Thomas Bonometti, vaun0815, Yana Yuzvenko, Zdeněk Macháček. and Mark Rise.

www.ingramcontent.com/pod-product-compliance
Lightning Source LLC
Chambersburg PA
CBHW040414220526
45473CB00004B/1234